A Book like no Other

Light for Your Path

The Light for Your Path Series is for women who desire to know, love, and serve God better. Each book is designed to nurture new believers while challenging women who are ready for deeper study. Studies in the series examine *books* of the Bible, on the one hand (look for subtitles beginning with *Light from*), and important *topics* in Christian faith and life, on the other (look for subtitles beginning with *Focus on*). The series blends careful instruction with active reader participation in a variety of study exercises, always encouraging women to live in the light of biblical truth in practical ways.

Two foundational studies explain why and how to study the Bible as the one perfect light source for your Christian walk:

A Book Like No Other: What's So Special About the Bible
Turning On the Light: Discovering the Riches of God's Word

A BOOK LIKE NO OTHER

What's So Special About the Bible

Carol J. Ruvolo

P U B L I S H I N G

P.O. BOX 817 • PHILLIPSBURG • NEW JERSEY 08865-0817

Unless otherwise indicated, Scripture quotations are from the New American Standard Bible. Copyright by the Lockman Foundation 1960, 1962, 1963, 1968, 1971, 1973, 1975, 1977. Italics indicate emphasis added.

Printed in the United States of America

Composition by Colophon Typesetting

Library of Congress Cataloging-in-Publication Data

Ruvolo, Carol J., 1946–
    A book like no other : what's so special about the Bible / Carol J. Ruvolo.
        p.   cm. — (Light for your path)
    Includes bibliographical references.
    ISBN 0-87552-627-6 (pbk.)
    1. Bible—Evidences, authority, etc. 2. Bible—Inspiration.
3. Reformed Church—Doctrines. I. Title. II. Series.
BS480.R85   1998
220.1—dc21   98-9905

*To the leaders of Providence Presbyterian Church
who have been appointed by God to watch over my soul.
To a man, they are bold, courageous, gentle servants
whose consistently high view of Scripture
holds me to the highest possible standard.*

CONTENTS

vii

The Light for Your Path Series

The Light for Your Path Series is designed to help women learn how to glorify and enjoy God by living out their transformation in Christ. Each book in the series reflects the author's commitment to the Bible as the infallible, inerrant, authoritative, and entirely sufficient Word of God, and her conviction that Reformed theology is the clearest and most accurate restatement of biblical truth.

The series begins with two foundational studies centering on the Bible itself. *A Book Like No Other: What's So Special About the Bible* presents (in six lessons) the unique character of God's revelation. *Turning On the Light: Discovering the Riches of God's Word* provides (in seven lessons) an effective approach to studying the Bible. Combining these two books in a thirteen-week course will prepare new and veteran students to gain the most from the Light for Your Path Series.

The remaining studies in the series fall into two categories. "Light" studies cover particular *books* of the Bible (or sections of books, or groups of books such as the Gospels). These studies guide you through portions of Scripture, enabling you to understand and apply the meaning of each passage. You will recognize them by their subtitles, beginning with the words *Light from*.

"Focus" studies spotlight important *topics* in the Christian faith and life, such as prayer, salvation, righteousness, and relationships, and seek to show what the whole Bible says about them. These studies also stress understanding and applying biblical truth in daily life. Their subtitles begin with the words *Focus on*. The *Leader's Guide* that accompanies this series contains a complete description of the purpose and format of these studies, along with helpful suggestions for leading women through them.

Studying a combination of biblical books and topics will shed much-needed scriptural light on your walk with God. Both types of Bible study should be included in a "balanced diet" for a growing Christian.

Bible study is a serious task that involves a significant investment of time and energy. Preparing yourself to study effectively will help you reap the greatest benefit from that investment. Study when you are well rested and alert. Try to find a time and place that is quiet, free of distractions, and conducive to concentration. Use a loose-leaf or spiral notebook to take notes on what you read and to do the exercises in this study. You may also want to develop a simple filing system so that you can refer to these notes in later studies.

Approach Bible study as you would any task that requires thought and effort to do well. Don't be surprised if it challenges you and stretches your thinking. Expect it to be difficult at times but extremely rewarding.

Always begin your study with prayer. Ask the Lord to reveal sin in your life that needs to be confessed and cleansed, to help you concentrate on His truths, and to illumine your mind with understanding of what He has written. End your study with a prayer for opportunities to apply what you have learned and wisdom to recognize those opportunities when they occur.

Each lesson in these studies is followed by three types of "Exercises": "Review," "Application," and "Digging Deeper." The *review* exercises will help you determine how well you understood the lesson material by giving you an opportunity to express the key points in your own words. The *application* exercises encourage you to put your understanding of the material to work in your daily life. And the *digging deeper* exercises challenge you to pursue further study in certain key areas.

You should be able to find the answers to the *review* questions in the lesson material itself, but please resist the temptation to copy words or phrases out of the lesson when you answer these questions. Work at putting these ideas into your own words. When you can do this, you know you have understood what you have read. It might help to ask yourself, "How would I explain this idea to someone else if I didn't have the book with me?"

If you don't have time to do all of the *application* exercises, pray over them and ask the Lord to show you which one(s) *He* wants you to work on. Because you will be applying the lessons to your daily life, these applications should take some time and thought. Answering one of them well will benefit you more than answering all of them superficially.

Answers to the application exercises should be very specific. Work at avoiding vague generalities. It might help to keep in mind that a specific application will answer the questions Who? What? When? Where? and How? A vague generality will not. You can make applications in the areas of your thinking, your attitudes, and your behavior. (See lesson 6 of *Turning On the Light* for more about application.)

Digging deeper exercises usually require a significant amount of time and effort to complete. They were designed to provide a challenge for mature Christians who are eager for more advanced study. However, new Christians should not automatically pass them by. The Holy Spirit may choose to use one of them to help you grow. Remember that *all Christians* grow by stretching beyond where they are right now. So if one or two of these exercises intrigue you, spend some time working on them. And, do not hesitate to ask for help from your pastor, elders, or more mature Christian friends.

As you work through this study, resist the temptation to compare yourself with other Christians in your group. The purpose of this study is to help you grow in your faith by learning and applying God's truth in your daily life—not to fill up a study book with brilliantly worded answers. If you learn and apply *one element* of God's truth in each lesson, you are consistently moving beyond where you were when you began.

Always remember that effective Bible study equips you *to glorify God and enjoy Him forever.* You glorify God when you live in such a way that those around you can look at you and see an accurate reflection of God's character and nature. You enjoy God when you are fully satisfied in His providential ordering of the circumstances in your life. When your life glorifies God and your joy is rooted in His providence, your impact on our fallen world will be tremendous.

ACKNOWLEDGMENTS

So many people have contributed to my understanding of the Bible as a Book like no other. My parents, John and Betty Boling, first introduced me to it. They taught me that it is a very special Book because every word in it came from God. They laid a rock-solid foundation upon which others have built.

My dear friends, Mark and Susie Menicucci, showed me not only that it is a very special Book from God, but also that its message applies to me—personally. With the testimony of their words and their lives, they introduced me to my Lord and Savior Jesus Christ—about whom that special Book is written.

More dear friends, Mike and Patti Lane, helped me understand its comprehensive sufficiency for every circumstance of life. They, perhaps more than anyone else, helped me understand and begin to live out my transformation in Jesus Christ.

A great many pastors, teachers, and writers (most of whom I have never met) have also come alongside me to broaden and deepen my understanding of God's very special Book. I am grateful to people like John Calvin, B. B. Warfield, Jonathan Edwards, Martyn Lloyd-Jones, Francis and Edith Schaeffer, A. W. Pink, James Montgomery Boice, R. C. Sproul, James I. Packer, Elisabeth Elliott, John MacArthur, Jr., Michael Horton, Jay Adams, David Wells, and my own pastor, Randy L. Steele, who have influenced me tremendously. Praise God for the commitment of these dedicated, godly saints!

My husband, Frank, and my daughter, Cinnamon, continue to bless me with time to study, and the women of Providence Presbyterian Church in Albuquerque encourage me in more ways than I can count.

And finally (last on the list but not in my heart), the patient, loving, God-fearing professionals at P&R Publishing, particularly

Barbara Lerch and Thom Notaro, have most assuredly been chosen of God to do critically important work. I simply cannot find the words to express how much I depend on and appreciate what they do.

But my deepest gratitude goes to the Lord God almighty who, for His own good pleasure, chose to reveal Himself to me through a Book. Thank you, Lord, for this astounding gift.

The written word of the Lord leads
us to the living Lord of the Word,
and our attitude to Him is effectively
our choice of destiny.
—J. I. Packer

The Preacher

The elegant old preacher gripped the edges of his magnificent teak pulpit and looked out over his impressive congregation. Almost two thousand well-groomed bodies rested comfortably in luxuriously up-holstered pews and directed their self-satisfied gaze toward their revered leader.

He had built this church from practically nothing. Seventy-five struggling parishioners had gathered to hear his first sermon almost thirty years ago, a sermon that told them exactly what they wanted to hear. Their tiny little church could grow—and would grow under his expert leadership. He came to them with impeccable theological credentials, coupled with the requisite managerial skills to lead them into the twenty-first century. He was the man who could take them from the relative insignificance they were so tired of to the stellar prominence they so greatly desired. The vote was sixty-seven to eight. Sixty-seven eager disciples chose to place their futures in his hands, and he had more than fulfilled their expectations.

His intelligent gray eyes scanned the spacious sanctuary and came to rest on a distressingly empty patch of burgundy upholstery. His wife of forty-three years had refused to accompany him this morning. His attempts to explain his change of heart had thoroughly embarrassed and confused her. She simply couldn't understand how the man who had built the most notable church in the city could have suddenly been "converted." When he tried to explain the stunning ramifications of his unexpected transformation, she decided he was experiencing a nervous breakdown and threatened to call her psychiatrist. She may have, for all he knew. The men in the white jackets could be waiting for him in the foyer right now.

But even if they were, he had no choice but to proceed. God had given him no other options. His impressive sheep in their comfortable fold were in grave danger. He was their shepherd, responsible for their care, and he had to warn them. Tightening his grip on the edge of the pulpit, he prayed silently as he opened his mouth to speak.

"My text for this morning is Jeremiah 23:29–32:

> *"Is not My word like fire?" declares the LORD, "and like a hammer which shatters a rock? Therefore behold, I am against the prophets," declares the LORD, "who steal My words from each other. Behold, I am against the prophets," declares the LORD, "who use their tongues and declare, 'The Lord declares.' Behold, I am against those who have prophesied false dreams," declares the LORD, "and related them, and led My people astray by their falsehoods and reckless boasting; yet I did not send them or command them, nor do they furnish this people the slightest benefit," declares the LORD.*

"Beloved, the fiery Word of God has shattered the rock that was my own heart and has brought me to my knees. I have sinned greatly against God and against you, my congregation. I have come to ask your forgiveness, and to call you to follow me in repentance, confession, and commitment to the truth of Scripture.

"I stand before you revealed as one of the prophets the Lord is against in this passage of Jeremiah. I have used my tongue to say to you 'The Lord declares' what the Lord has not declared. I have prophesied falsely. I have led you astray. The Lord did not send me to you to do this, but I ran to you of my own accord to bring you these lies. And I have not furnished you the slightest benefit in thirty years of ministry.

"God has shown me my sin, given me the grace to repent of it, and commissioned me to call upon you, my congregation, to repudiate the things I have taught you in the past. I have promised the Lord that, to the best of my ability, I will teach nothing in this place from this day forward that is not fully consistent with His inspired, inerrant,

and infallible Word, the Bible, and I am imploring you to follow me in this commitment."

— — —

The elegant old preacher went on to deliver a powerful sermon exposing the sham of his previous ministry by holding it up to the light of the Bible. Six months later, he was preaching to one hundred and fifty convicted sinners who were meeting in their fellowship hall and waiting for their spacious sanctuary to sell.

The consensus of local public opinion decreed that the old preacher's approach to his congregation had been much too drastic. He should have realized that such antiquated preaching would scare people off and destroy the church he had worked so hard to build. What local public opinion failed to understand (indeed has never understood) is that Christianity *is* drastic. God's righteous holiness demands that drastic action be taken against sin.

As the Holy Spirit illumined the old preacher's understanding of Scripture, he learned how drastic the separation was between him and His God, and how drastic was the extension of God's grace to the elect. When the preacher recognized himself in the book of Jeremiah, his guilt and remorse moved him to drastic action. He wrote his resignation and prepared to live out his days in secluded contrition. God, however, refused to let him off so easily.

Further study, under the convicting tutelage of the Holy Spirit, revealed his responsibility to his flock and compelled him to take yet more drastic action. He had to go to his people in repentance, confess his sin, ask their forgiveness, and implore them to join him in returning to the authority of God's Word. God's words to the prophet in Jeremiah 1:9–10 gave him clear direction and a small measure of comfort.

> Behold, I have put My words in your mouth.
> See, I have appointed you this day over the nations and
>   over the kingdoms,
> *To pluck up and to break down,*
> *To destroy and to overthrow,*
> To build and to plant.

The preacher understood for the first time why Jeremiah has been dubbed the "weeping prophet." The message he carried to Israel was drastic. Before he could build and plant, he would have to pluck up, break down, destroy, and overthrow. The elegant old preacher faced the same challenges. Before he could begin planting the truth in the hearts of the people he had led astray, before he could lay a solid foundation upon which they could build, he faced the chore of demolition. The hardy weeds of godless theology and the towering edifice of humanistic philosophy had to be destroyed. This would be all the more difficult for him, because he had planted those hardy weeds and built that towering edifice himself.

He took comfort from Paul's words recorded in Romans 5:20–21: "But where sin increased, grace abounded all the more, that, as sin reigned in death, even so grace might reign through righteousness to eternal life through Jesus Christ our Lord." He knew that only God's abounding grace could overcome the sin he had allowed to increase to such proportions among his own sheep.

As we begin our study of God's Word, a Book like no other, we will inevitably find ourselves involved in the work of demolition—just like the elegant old preacher. And that should not surprise us. All of us have been influenced to some degree by false teaching and worldly pollution. All of us have allowed weeds to flourish in the gardens of our minds and have worshiped at shrines dedicated to false philosophies. Part of learning truth is uncovering error.

The only way we will effectively learn truth is to pay diligent heed to the Word of Truth, the Bible. The reason Christians are so easily led astray by error is that they have failed to attend to the Scriptures. As I was preparing to write this Bible study, I kept coming across authors who voiced concern over "modern" (and "postmodern") Christianity's view of the Bible. Christians themselves seem to be drifting dangerously far from their once-secure moorings of commitment to absolute truth. As they do so, they are becoming increasingly accepting of godless theologies and humanistic philosophies.

James Montgomery Boice, in his book *Standing on the Rock,* says that there is no firm view of truth these days. He explains that most modern people, including a great many Christian leaders, have accepted the Hegelian view of history,[1] which denies the existence of absolute truth. The result has been a dramatic shift in preaching from an authoritative proclamation of God's truth to an anemic presentation of friendly suggestions, accompanied by an inevitable decline in personal holiness and Christian witness.[2]

J. I. Packer addresses the same issue by describing an unhealthy church that staggers on "from gimmick to gimmick and stunt to stunt like so many drunks in a fog, not knowing at all where we are or which way we should be going."[3] He acknowledges that the Bible is being studied and read a great deal, but not as the infallible Word of the living God. Liberal "scholarship" has driven a wedge between *revelation* (the Word of God to us) and *the Bible* (man's written witness to the Word of God to us). Because the Bible is no longer viewed as identical with revelation, Christians cannot rely on it to provide a ground of certainty for their faith. And so, they are looking elsewhere.[4]

John F. MacArthur recounts the tragic story of Homer and Langley Collyer, eccentric millionaire brothers who, refusing to avail themselves of the fabulous wealth at their disposal, lived wretchedly and died tragically amid squalid conditions. He goes on to compare the way many Christians live their spiritual lives to the way Homer and Langley lived their physical lives.

> Disregarding the bountiful riches of an inheritance that cannot be defiled (1 Pet. 1:4), they scour the wreckage of worldly wisdom, collecting litter. As if the riches of God's grace (Eph. 1:7) were not enough, as if "everything pertaining to life and godliness" (2 Pet. 1:3) were not sufficient, they try to supplement the resources that are theirs in Christ. They spend their lives pointlessly accumulating sensational experiences, novel teachings, clever gurus, or whatever else they can find to add to their hoard of spiritual experiences. Practically all of it is utterly worthless. Yet some people pack themselves so full of these diversions that they can't find the door to the truth that would set them free. They forfeit treasure for trash.[5]

The board of directors of Soli Deo Gloria Publications, in the preface of their book *Sola Scriptura!,* defines the primary question governing our relationship with God to be whether we submit ourselves to His revelation or to our own imaginations.[6] And Neil Postman, the insightful critic, writer, educator, and communications theorist, warns that "we are people on the verge of amusing ourselves to death."[7]

The testimony of these godly men (and many others) reaffirmed my concerns and validated my desire to write this study. Not only do I see a real need for Christians in general to recapture an orthodox devotion to the Bible as the inspired, authoritative, and fully sufficient Word of God, but I also see a need for women in particular to do so. Why? Because women have a vital role to play in reversing this disastrous trend among modern Christians, and because we are so easily tempted "to leave such things to the men."

We tend to underestimate our impact as mothers, wives, friends, and coworkers; and to forget that God has placed us in key situations to testify solemnly of the gospel of the grace of God (Acts 20:24). We must conscientiously prepare ourselves to give an answer to those who ask us the reason for the hope that we have in Him (1 Peter 3:15–16)—and that includes learning how to defend our confidence in God's unique revelation, the Bible.

We are responsible to teach our children wisely, advise our husbands respectfully, and compassionately help our friends and coworkers understand the great truths of Scripture. As we pursue the affairs of our daily lives, we touch people with whom "the men" will never come in contact.

Many of you work with people your pastor has never met. Many of you, while running errands and chauffeuring children, talk to people your husband doesn't know. Some of you live in apartment complexes, dormitories, sorority houses, or nursing homes primarily in the company of other women. Most of you have children who don't always ask their spiritual questions when Daddy is home to answer them, and some of you have children who don't have daddies to ask.

I hope I have made my point. Women need to be encouraged to study and learn the great truths of God. The opportunities God has given us to declare those truths must not be wasted. We must begin with the Book. We must know why we revere and honor it as the sole source of absolute truth if we are to lay a firm foundation for the hope that we have, and we must be able to explain that hope to others.

We mustn't yield to the temptation to leave it to the men. They can't do it all. God doesn't expect them to.

Notes

1. Hegel taught that history moves through a process of struggle and resolution. Accepted truths are inevitably challenged by alternative truths that eventually produce new truth. He used the terms *thesis, antithesis,* and *synthesis* to describe this process. In his philosophy, truth cannot be absolute because it is constantly evolving.

2. James M. Boice, *Standing on the Rock* (Grand Rapids: Baker, 1994), 15–19.

3. J. I. Packer, *God Has Spoken* (Grand Rapids: Baker, 1979), 20.

4. Ibid., 28.

5. John MacArthur, Jr., *Our Sufficiency in Christ* (Dallas: Word, 1991), 38–39.

6. Don Kistler, ed., *Sola Scriptura!: The Protestant Position on the Bible* (Morgan, Pa.: Soli Deo Gloria, 1995), x.

7. Neil Postman, *Amusing Ourselves to Death* (New York: Penguin, 1985), 4.

1

The Problem of Truth Decay

"Behold, days are coming," declares the Lord GOD,
"When I will send a famine on the land,
Not a famine for bread or a thirst for water,
But rather for hearing the words of the LORD.
And people will stagger from sea to sea,
And from the north even to the east;
They will go to and fro to seek the word of the LORD,
But they will not find it." —Amos 8:11–12

Several years ago, my sister moved from one small South Carolina town to another and began a surprisingly difficult search for a church to attend. A few weeks into her search, she called me to vent a little of her accumulated frustration, and I have never forgotten one comment she made: "I walked into one adult Sunday school class and crossed another church off my list. I was the only person in the room with a Bible!"

We had a good laugh, but the situation she described was far from funny. That church was exhibiting one of the primary symptoms of "truth decay," a frequently fatal malady that occurs, according to Michael Horton, when God's words are replaced by human words.[1] No one in that adult Sunday school class was carrying a Bible because God's words were no longer important to them. They preferred listening to each other.

I have attended similarly ill churches that exhibited a slightly different symptom of the same disease. In these churches, people actually carry Bibles—and read them. But they also replace God's words with human words. "Bible study" in these churches amounts to reading a verse out of context and going around the room sharing "what this verse means to me." No one cares about what God had in mind when He wrote the verse, but each one is eager to explain what he or she had in mind when reading it.

Prophetic Voices

The problem of truth decay is spreading rapidly in twentieth-century Christianity, but that should not come as a surprise to any of us. The prophet Amos described it quite accurately over twenty-seven hundred years ago when he predicted a coming famine in the land: "not a famine for bread or a thirst for water, but rather for hearing the words of the LORD" (Amos 8:11). He described a time when people would stagger from sea to sea and from north to east, seeking the word of the Lord, but would be unable to find it (v. 12).

Roughly one hundred years later, the prophet Jeremiah reiterated the message of his predecessor to a people who had grown increasingly insensitive to God's words. The warnings we find in the prophecies of Amos and Jeremiah were directed, in their immediate context, to the children of Israel, whose idolatrous adoption of false religious beliefs and practices was hurtling them toward the inevitable judgment of God.

God's covenant people had ignored His Word, embraced the godless philosophies and behavior of pagan cultures, and as a result, were suffering the systemic effects of truth decay. Seemingly insignificant defections from truth to error took hold in the body of Israel and multiplied relentlessly until every part was infected. Israel was sick—very sick.

God repeatedly commissioned faithful prophets to carry His words to His people and to plead with them to acknowledge their condition, repudiate their self-destructive habits, and seek healing from their God. However, His warnings consistently fell upon deaf ears. Israel paid a high price for her stubborn insensitivity as the blessings she had enjoyed as God's most-favored-nation evaporated in harsh captivity.

Déjà Vu All Over Again

Every time I read the prophecies of the Old Testament, particularly those of Jeremiah, I am struck by how relevant they are to our own age. The church in the twentieth century is blindly following in Israel's footsteps, and desperately needs to heed the warnings she ignored. God's description of His people Israel in the book of Jeremiah bears an uncanny resemblance to modern Christianity.

> My people have changed their glory
> For that which does not profit . . .
> For My people have committed two evils:
> They have forsaken Me,
> The fountain of living waters,
> To hew for themselves cisterns,
> Broken cisterns,
> That cannot hold water. (Jeremiah 2:11, 13)

> This people has a stubborn and rebellious heart;
> They have turned aside and departed.
> They do not say in their heart,
> "Let us now fear the LORD our God." (Jeremiah
>   5:23–24)

The vast majority of Christians in our day fear men much more than they fear God. They are more concerned about losing their safety, security, and self-esteem than they are about incurring the righteous wrath of their Creator. They are so absorbed in worldly pursuits that they have no time for the pursuit of God. Their self-centered preoccupation with the ways of the world makes them easy prey for false teachers who tickle their ears to feed their own greed.

Health and wealth proponents, pop psychologists, and a dazzling array of secularly credentialed experts bombard God's people with *everything but* the Word of God. After all, *human words* produce the desired results. Human words draw huge crowds. They stimulate growth. They bring in vast sums of money.

These modern-day false prophets are really not all that modern. Jeremiah knew all about them.

> For wicked men are found among My people,
> They watch like fowlers lying in wait;
> They set a trap,
> They catch men. . . .
> An appalling and horrible thing
> Has happened in the land:
> The prophets prophesy falsely,
> And the priests rule on their own authority;
> And my people love it so! (Jeremiah 5:26, 30–31)

> For from the least of them even to the greatest of
> them,
> Everyone is greedy for gain,
> And from the prophet even to the priest
> Everyone deals falsely.
> And they have healed the brokenness of My people
> superficially,
> Saying, "Peace, Peace,"
> But there is no peace.
> Were they ashamed because of the abomination they
> have done?
> They were not even ashamed at all;
> They did not even know how to blush. (Jeremiah
> 6:13–15)

Israel was ill and in desperate need of healing. Her leaders, instead of helping her recover, took advantage of her weakness for their own personal gain. They displayed themselves as spiritual healers, but were, in reality, nothing more than religious quacks. The situation is not all that different today. God's people are crowding aboard the Charlatan Express because they care more about enjoying the ride than they do about where they are going.

I Know! I Know!

When I was in the fourth grade, there was one kid in my class who knew all the answers. No matter what the teacher asked, she was hopping up and down in her seat waving her arm and yelling, "I know! I know!" She created such a disturbance, she was hard to ignore, but we all (including the teacher) tried our best to ignore her. Jeremiah reminds me of that little girl. He knew the answers. He wasn't shy about letting everyone know he knew the answers. He created such a disturbance, he was hard to ignore. But those around him did their best to ignore him.

This sorry state of affairs broke his heart. Jeremiah knew where the false prophets were headed and agonized over the heedless abandon with which God's people were following them to destruction.

> My sorrow is beyond healing,
> My heart is faint within me!
> Behold, listen! The cry of the daughter of my people
> from a distant land:
> "Is the Lord not in Zion? Is her King not within her?"
> "Why have they provoked Me with their graven images,
> with foreign idols?"
> "Harvest is past, summer is ended,
> And we are not saved."
> For the brokenness of the daughter of my people I am
> broken;
> I mourn, dismay has taken hold of me.
> Is there no balm in Gilead?
> Is there no physician there?
> Why then has not the health of the daughter of my
> people been restored? (Jeremiah 8:18–22)

Those who stand in Jeremiah's shoes today and call God's people to heed His truth weep just as easily as he did and ask the same kinds of questions. Why are God's people so easily deceived? Why are they so gullible? Why are they so quick to believe lies, and so slow to believe the truth? The questions are the same—and the answer is the same. Because they don't know their God. And they don't know their God because they don't know His Word. And they don't know His Word because they don't attend to it. "Truth decay" is, by and large, a disease of neglect and indifference, and can only be healed by attention and concern. Jeremiah knew this. He learned it by listening to God.

> Thus says the Lord, "Let not a wise man boast of his wisdom, and let not the mighty man boast of his might, let not a rich man boast of his riches; but let him who boasts boast of this, that he understands and knows Me, that I am the LORD who exercises lovingkindness, justice, and righteousness on earth; for I delight in these things," declares the LORD. (Jeremiah 9:23–24)

If the church is to learn from Israel's mistakes, we must cultivate a love for God's words. The only way to escape the famine in the land is to develop an appetite for scriptural truth. We must consult our God; we must direct our attention to the Word and to "the testimony" (Isaiah 8:20). And, we must not deceive ourselves by thinking it will be easy. It won't be.

We live in a culture that largely denies the very idea of absolute truth. We worship with believers who have been influenced by that culture more than they realize. We ourselves have been influenced more than we realize. Perhaps now more than ever, directing our attention to Scripture necessitates swimming *against* swift-running cultural currents. The effort promises to be exhausting.

Let Me Draw You a Picture

The familiar adage "A picture is worth a thousand words" has never been truer than it is today. Culturally we have become a visually oriented people. Given a choice, we would much rather see the movie than read the book. God, however, did not reveal His truth on video tape; He wrote a Book. And we can be sure He chose this method of revelation for a very good reason.

Neil Postman, in his insightful book *Amusing Ourselves to Death,* explains why. The *medium* of communication, Postman says, determines to a large degree the kind of information it can communicate. Certain forms of communication necessarily exclude certain types of content. Smoke signals, for example, cannot be used to transmit profound philosophical arguments. Writing, on the other hand, encourages and facilitates the highest levels of thinking.[2]

God's decision to reveal Himself and His truth in and through His *written* Word reflects the mind-engaging, conceptual character of His revelation. He even went so far as to forbid replacing the Word with an image, and thus condemned the inevitable idolatry that accompanies the shift from a word-oriented religion to an image-oriented one.

The validity of God's prohibition is evident in our culture. As we have moved from being a word-oriented people to an image-oriented people, our Christianity has suffered. When Americans were accustomed to structuring their political, societal, and educational lives around reading and writing, they naturally structured their religious lives around the Bible. But as print media gave way to picture media, Bibles were laid aside and ignored. Americans are out of the habit of reading. They have developed a television mentality that devours information in thirty-second, easy-to-swallow sound bites. Pausing to chew simply requires too much effort.

Christianity, however, requires chewing. Holiness cannot be pursued with a television mentality. Godliness cannot be practiced without thinking. Faith does not come by entertainment; it comes by hearing the Word of God (Romans 10:17).

If we are going to hear the Word of God, we are going to have to read it—and think about it. We are going to have to buck the culture. We are going to have to tear down edifices glorifying fun and games, and pull up weeds planted by fallen desire. We are going to have to turn off the television, sacrifice some comfort, and make an effort to chew thoroughly. We will not be entertained, but we will be edified.

I am ready to begin, and I hope you are too. Let's get started.

Notes

1. See the foreword by Michael Horton in Don Kistler, ed., *Sola Scriptura!: The Protestant Position on the Bible* (Morgan, Pa.: Soli Deo Gloria, 1995).

2. Neil Postman, *Amusing Ourselves to Death* (New York: Penguin, 1985), 4–9. Postman's book analyzes the impact of television on American culture and reveals much of what, I believe, is at the root of modern Christianity's infatuation with the world. I encourage every Christian to read this important book thoughtfully and prayerfully!

Exercises

Review

1. Describe the problem of "truth decay."

2. Describe Israel's spiritual condition at the time when Amos and Jeremiah were called by God to prophesy. Do you see any similarities between Israel's spiritual condition at that time and the spiritual condition of the church today? Explain.

3. What made Jeremiah's attitude toward the people of Israel different from the attitude of the false prophets toward them? How might understanding this difference help you distinguish between true and false teachers today?

4. Read Psalm 19:7–12, Isaiah 8:19–20, Jeremiah 23:29, Romans 10:17, and Hebrews 2:1–4. What do these verses teach about the solution to the problem of truth decay?

5. Distinguish between a word-oriented culture and a picture-oriented one. Why is this distinction important?

Application

1. Describe any personal encounters you have had with churches or religious groups that were suffering from "truth decay." Did you recognize the problem at the time? If not, when did you first

recognize the problem and what caused you to recognize it? How did you respond when you recognized the problem? Do you believe your response was edifying to those who were afflicted with truth decay? Was it edifying to you? Did it glorify God? Explain.

2. Read through the book of Amos and the first nine chapters of Jeremiah. Ask God to show you at least one passage that reveals an attitude or an action of yours toward His Word that you need to change. Record the passage you find, and describe the change you need to make. Then write out a detailed plan to accomplish the needed change.

3. Are you primarily word-oriented or picture-oriented? (If you are not sure, try recording the amount of time you spend watching television and movies versus the amount of time you spend reading.) How does your basic orientation affect your interaction with God's Word? Do you need to make any changes in this area of your life? If so, describe the changes and explain how you will go about accomplishing them.

4. Are you ready to commit yourself to *hearing* the Word of God by reading and studying it? If so, write out your commitment.

Digging Deeper

1. Study the first nine chapters of Jeremiah. Do some research on the history of Israel to help you understand the political, cultural, and religious situation in the nation at the time of Jeremiah's prophecy. Do you believe that Jeremiah's words in the first nine chapters are as relevant for twentieth-century Christians as they were for the people in his own day? If you do, explain the similarities between our culture and Jeremiah's, and describe how modern Christians should heed his words.

2. Purchase or borrow a copy of Neil Postman's book, *Amusing Ourselves to Death*. Read the book carefully, and write a critical review of it, pointing out why you agree or disagree with his views.

2

How Do You Know?

I wonder whence the Scriptures should come, if not from God. Bad men could not be the authors of it. Would their minds be employed in indicting such holy lines? Would they declare so fiercely against sin? Could good men be the authors of it? Could they write in such a strain? Or could it stand with their grace to counterfeit God's name and put "Thus saith the Lord" to a book of their own devising? —Thomas Watson

Probability is not . . . the guide of life. —Cornelius Van Til

My brother-in-law is a professional journalist. He is skilled in the art of gathering information relevant to a particular issue, critically evaluating it, and reaching supportable conclusions. His professional training permeates his entire life and naturally colored the way he responded to the Holy Spirit's effectual call to salvation. His awakening interest in spiritual things precipitated a thorough "investigation" of religion. True to form, he began his quest by talking to a wide assortment of religious people—Hindus, Buddhists, Mormons, Moslems, Jews, and Christians—and by reading an even wider assortment of holy books.

Knowing of my deep commitment to Christianity, he "interviewed" me over lunch one day. One of his questions was partic-ularly insightful. "All of these religions make blatant claims to be the truth," he said. "They all claim to be from God. Yet because they differ, they can't all be true. *How do you know* Christianity is true?"

I knew my brother-in-law wouldn't be satisfied with easy an-swers such as "I just know in my heart it's true" or "Jesus changed my life." He already had a file folder full of emotional experien-tial endorsements from countless devotees of scores of religions. What he wanted to know was if Christianity was any different from the rest.

I told him (in a remarkably short period of time) everything I knew about apologetics,[1] loaned him my well-worn copy of C. S. Lewis's little classic, *Mere Christianity,* and prayed like mad! He lis-tened to me quietly and promised to read the book. Several months later, he pulled me aside at a family dinner and told me he had become a Christian. The Holy Spirit had been pleased to use my stumbling words and C. S. Lewis's eloquent ones to show him that Christianity is indeed different from the rest.

What's the Difference?

The Book that tells us about Christianity is also different from the rest—truly a Book like no other. The Bible displays certain unique qualities that identify it as the only Book in man's library written by God. It is the only Holy Book that embodies absolute truth. In this Book, and only in this Book, God communicates His special revelation to us. Only by understanding the message of this Book can we acquire a full and true knowledge of God.

At the time my brother-in-law questioned me about Christian-ity, he was what a pastor-friend of mine calls an "elect unbeliever." I would broaden that definition a bit and describe him as an "en-lightened" elect unbeliever. God was working in his life to draw him to Himself and graciously allowing him to travel toward the king-dom on a familiar road—the road of intellectual investigation.

He had reached a major roadblock in his path—an incredible assortment of truth claims, all clamoring for his attention—and he was looking for a way to efficiently clear the road and get on with his journey. His question to me amounted to asking, "Which of these claims should I toss into the ditch, and which ones should I investigate more thoroughly?"

My job, at that point, was not to *convince* him of Christianity's validity, but to focus his attention on the Bible. I did this by acquainting him with the *evidence* for the Bible's uniqueness so that he would see it as the most likely candidate for closer scrutiny. Once he actually began reading it under the illuminating power of the Holy Spirit, God did the rest.

Presenting the Evidence

The evidence supporting the Bible's uniqueness abounds. The apostle Peter was not making an unreasonable demand when he admonished Christians to be ready always "to make a defense to everyone who asks you to give an account for the hope that is in you . . ." (1 Peter 3:15). We should never hesitate to defend our faith. The overwhelming preponderance of evidence supports our case.

However, most of us do much more than hesitate. We disintegrate. All it takes is one serious challenge to our faith to completely unnerve us. We backpedal furiously, stumble over our words, stare at our extremities in embarrassed silence, or run to get our pastor. We act this way because we have either wrongly accepted responsibility for convincing our challenger of the truth or suddenly realized we are not very well acquainted with the evidence supporting our beliefs.

Becoming an effective defender of the faith involves, first of all, understanding that we cannot convince an unbeliever that the Bible is the Word of God or persuade him to become a Christian. Only God can do that. John Calvin expressed it this way: "For as God alone is a fit witness of himself in his world, so also the Word will not find acceptance in men's hearts before it is sealed by the inward testimony of the Spirit."[2]

The "natural man" does not accept the truths of God because he does not have the ability to do so. Understanding the truths of God requires spiritual insight that unredeemed men and women do not have. Until they are given this insight by the Holy Spirit,

God's truth appears foolish to them (1 Corinthians 2:14). This is why unbelievers continue to reject the divine authorship of the Bible and the validity of the Christian faith even in the face of sound, reasonable evidence.

That does not mean, however, that we should not present the evidence to unbelievers. We should prepare ourselves to share the abundant evidence for Christian truth for four very good reasons:

(1) It demonstrates the superiority of the Christian faith over other religions.
(2) It elicits objections from unbelievers, thereby exposing a pattern of resistance to God's Word and illustrating that unbelief is essentially a tendency of the heart to fight God.
(3) When we interpret evidence in the light of Scripture, it serves as a medium for conveying biblical truth, which generates faith.
(4) It often stimulates "enlightened elect unbelievers" to study the Bible for themselves.

The next time you are confronted by a skeptic, don't back away for fear of not being able to convince him you are right. That's not your job. Your job is to present the evidence as clearly as you can, and trust God to use your efforts to accomplish His purposes.

No Shortage of Evidence

Before you can present that evidence, however, you have to become familiar with it yourself. In order to do that, you will have to invest some of your scarcest natural resources (time and energy) in concentrated study. But you can also rest assured that your costly investment will produce a highly profitable spiritual return.

We are limited by time and space to a brief overview of the evidence for Scripture's divine origin and Christianity's validity, but I hope this small taste of apologetics will whet your appetite for further study.[3]

Experiential Evidence. This is the quickest and easiest evidence to provide, but it is also the weakest. Recounting how the

Bible made an impact on you and how Jesus changed your life Is extremely relevant—to you. However, your listener has probably heard the same story from committed disciples of Buddha, Ghandi, Karl Marx, aerobic exercise, and anti-depressant drugs!

We tend to fall back on this kind of evidence because it is safe. No one can successfully argue against your personal experiences. This kind of evidence rarely (if ever) precipitates threatening disagreements or relationship-shattering face-offs. It fosters tolerance and goodwill even among people of differing opinions. However, unless your testimony centers on the unique message of the gospel and not merely your experience of happiness, this type of evidence is no different from other religions and does not elevate the Bible as the only source of absolute truth. It's one thing to talk about how much happier you are now. It's quite another to express your inability to dodge the Bible's message that you are at heart a sinner and that God had to send Someone from out of this world—His own Son—to save you. That kind of experiential evidence lifts the Christian experience above all others by focusing on the essential heart issues.

The Unity of the Bible. This kind of evidence focuses the inquirer's attention directly on the Bible by describing some of its unique characteristics. The Bible is the only book in existence that was written over a period of fifteen hundred years by more than forty authors in sixty-six distinct segments and yet maintains a coherent, unified theme throughout. The Bible tells one single story of divine redemption conceived in eternity past, initiated at Creation, nurtured in the people of Israel, fulfilled in Jesus Christ, and eventually culminating in eternity future. Such a Book could not have been written without the services of a Divine Editor.

Evidence such as this quickly sets the Bible apart from other holy books and provides an excellent springboard for evangelism. Once you have told your inquirer that the Bible records one coherent story from beginning to end, you can move quite naturally into telling that story and presenting your inquirer with his lost condition and need for salvation.

This is virtually the only evidence I presented to my brother-in-law at lunch that day—because at the time, it was all I knew. But

God blessed it by piquing his interest and stimulating him to further study. The time I had spent learning even this much was definitely well-spent!

The Accuracy of the Bible. This is another line of evidence that draws the inquirer's attention to the unique character of Scripture. When we view the Bible as the only source of absolute truth written by the sovereign God of the universe, we expect everything written in it to be scientifically and historically accurate as well as spiritually beneficial—and that expectation is supported by the evidence.

The Bible is completely consistent with verifiable scientific principles such as the first and second laws of thermodynamics, the water cycle, the vastness of the universe, the circularity and movement of the earth, and the life-sustaining work of blood in the human body. Modern historians and archeologists also verify the Bible's accuracy in their fields of inquiry.

The Bible is not a complete textbook in any of these fields. It was not written for that purpose. But because its Author created and controls the natural world that humans investigate, His scientific and historical comments recorded in the Bible are always accurate.

When we present this type of evidence, we need to be careful *not* to give the impression that we are proving the Bible by supposedly *neutral* scientific and historical data. We must, instead, present the Bible as special revelation from the living God and express our confident expectations of its accuracy in these areas. Sharing the evidence reflecting the reasonableness of our expectations sets the Bible apart from all other holy books and glorifies God and His Word before the world.

Miracles and Prophecy. The same line of reasoning applies here. Because God wrote the Bible, we expect the prophecies it contains to be perfectly fulfilled and the miracles recorded there to defy "natural" explanation. However, without the intervening work of the Holy Spirit, no appeal to fulfilled prophecy or astounding miracles as proof of Christianity will convert an unbeliever.

I learned that rather forcefully not long after I became a Christian. After reading Josh McDowell's excellent little book, *The Resurrection Factor,* I thought I finally had all the evidence I needed to convert my husband to Christianity. As soon as he walked in the door that night, I asked him point-blank, "If I could convince you that the resurrection of Jesus Christ actually happened, would you accept Him as your Savior?" He replied with an equally point-blank, No.

All the evidence in the world cannot convince a dead person to breathe. Jesus illustrated this truth in His parable of the rich man and Lazarus (see Luke 16:19–31). When the rich man in his agony begged Father Abraham to send someone back from the dead to testify to his brothers, Abraham replied, "If they do not listen to Moses and the Prophets, neither will they be persuaded if someone rises from the dead" (v. 31).

Again, the purpose behind presenting the evidence of fulfilled prophecies and miraculous events is to focus the inquirer's attention on God's special revelation recorded in the Bible. The words of Scripture illumined by the Holy Spirit are alone effective in producing saving faith.

The Testimony of Jesus Christ. This is the very best evidence for the divine authorship of the Bible and the validity of Christianity, but one that your inquiring friends (and enemies) may have a hard time understanding until they have accepted the Bible as a reliable historical document.

Equipping yourself to present the Bible as a reliable historical document[4] will help them accept the historical record of the life and teaching of Jesus Christ. Encouraging them to evaluate the life and teaching of Jesus Christ as historical truth will help them see that this evidence supports His claims of deity. Once Jesus' deity is accepted, He becomes an unimpeachable authority on every topic He addresses, one of which is the divine authorship of the Bible. Therefore, on the testimony of Jesus Christ alone, elect unbelievers can confidently accept the Bible as God's written revelation to humanity.

Being able to defend your faith using the kind of evidence presented here is extremely important. Even though evidential arguments alone are insufficient to bring about conversion, they honor

God by exalting His Word above other religious books, and they may also be used by the Holy Spirit to introduce inquirers to the Bible itself, whose words alone *are* sufficient to quicken the dead to eternal life.

The Truth, the Whole Truth, and Nothing but the Truth

A few of my Christian friends experienced what amounted to a crisis of faith when they learned that the Bible they cherish came into being through the work of various church councils.[5] They immediately began asking questions like, "How do we know they picked the right books?" and "How do we know they didn't leave some out?" I think they would have been happier believing that the Bible as we know it—all sixty-six books bound in genuine cowhide—dropped complete from heaven into the apostle Paul's lap with a note from the Lord saying, "This is My Word. Teach from it."

God did not choose to give us His Word that way, even though He could have. He chose instead to work through means—the means of human authors writing under the inspiration of the Holy Spirit (2 Peter 1:20–21). We will discuss the process of inspiration in lesson 3, but before we do, we need to take a brief look at how the early church fathers identified those inspired writings.

In a word, they identified them by *recognizing* them for what they were. The church did not decide on its own authority which books were to be included in the Canon (the word used to refer to the complete list of inspired writings included in the Bible). God, acting on His authority alone, decided which books would be included in His Scripture when He ordained and appointed the prophets and apostles who would record His truth under the inspiration of His Spirit. That same Spirit then illumined the hearts and minds of the early church fathers to recognize and identify those writings. J. I. Packer aptly states that the early church did not give us the canon of Scripture any more than Sir Isaac Newton gave us the force of gravity.[6] Sir Isaac and the early church simply recognized and identified what God had already done.

The process of identifying canonical writings took some time. It was not until A.D. 397 at the Third Council of Carthage that all the writings included in our Bible today were recognized as canonical.[7] The godly men putting their heads together at that council were guided by three Spirit-given criteria for deciding which books would be included in the Bible: (1) apostolic authorship or authorization (Luke, for instance, was not an apostle, but his writing is validated as Scripture by the apostle Paul in 1 Timothy 5:18.), (2) acceptance by the original churches as Scripture, and (3) consistency with the undisputed core of established Scripture.

We can be certain that God exercised sovereign control over the work of these men as they labored to give us the Bible. Bringing the inspired writings of the prophets and apostles together in one Book was an essential element in God's ongoing plan to communicate His truth to His people, and He would not allow that process to fail.

A People of the Book

Christians are accurately called a people of the Book. Everything we believe and everything we are rests on God's revelation in the Bible. If the Bible is not reliable, Christianity goes out the window. Benjamin B. Warfield has said that without a trustworthy Bible, the soul is left without sure ground for proper knowledge of itself, its condition, its need, and a proper knowledge of God's provision of mercy and promise of grace.[8] Our eternal destiny depends on the attention we pay to the Bible, for unless we heed its message, we cannot be saved from eternal damnation.

Those of us who have already placed our trust in Christ for salvation must also heed the Bible's message, for it tells us how to live according to our high calling in Christ. Failure to attend to Scripture cripples our ability to walk worthy of our calling and robs God of the glory He deserves and demands.

One of the best ways to assure that we give proper attention to Scripture is to keep in mind its essential character and not forget what a treasure it is. The lessons that follow will help us to understand what is so special about the Bible.

Notes

1. "Apologetics" is a subdivision of Christian theology concerned with defending the divine origin and authority of the Christian faith.

2. John Calvin, *Institutes of the Christian Religion,* ed. John T. McNeill, 2 vols. (Philadelphia: Westminster Press, 1960), 1:79.

3. There are many excellent books on the market dealing with apologetics. I would recommend for beginners, Josh McDowell, *Evidence That Demands a Verdict,* and Richard L. Pratt, Jr., *Every Thought Captive.* For those who are ready to do some serious chewing in this area, I recommend the work of John Frame and Cornelius Van Til.

4. The information in chapter 4 of Josh McDowell's *Evidence That Demands a Verdict* will help you present the Bible as a reliable historical document.

5. Students interested in an exhaustive treatment of the development of the Bible as we know it today may refer to F. F. Bruce, *The Canon of Scripture* (Downers Grove, Ill.: InterVarsity Press, 1988).

6. J. I. Packer, *God Has Spoken* (Grand Rapids: Baker, 1979), 119.

7. R. C. Sproul, "The Establishment of Scripture," in *Sola Scriptura!: The Protestant Position on the Bible,* ed. Don Kistler (Morgan, Pa.: Soli Deo Gloria, 1995), 75.

8. Benjamin B. Warfield, *The Inspiration and Authority of the Bible,* ed. Samuel B. Craig (Philadelphia: Presbyterian and Reformed, 1948), 124.

Exercises

Review

1. How is the Bible different from every other religious book in the world?

2. Why is understanding the message of the Bible important? (Explain why it is important for an "elect unbeliever" and for an "elect believer.")

3. What is your primary responsibility to someone who asks you about your faith? What is the primary purpose for knowing how to "defend your faith"?

4. What impression must we avoid when presenting evidence such as biblical accuracy in scientific matters, miracles, and fulfilled prophecies? Why should we avoid giving such an impression?

5. How did the Canon of Scripture come into being?

6. List the criteria used by the church fathers at the Third Council of Carthage to identify the writings that should be included in our Bible. Why was each of these criteria essential in that process?

Application

1. Describe a time when someone asked you about your reasons for being a Christian. How did you respond to him or her? Did your response encourage your inquirer to investigate the Bible as the source of absolute truth? Given the opportunity, would you respond differently to that person today?

2. Study 1 Peter 3:13–16 along with 1 Corinthians 2:11–16. How does your study of these passages impact your understanding of evangelism? What changes do you need to make in the way you approach evangelism based on these passages?

3. Describe *and* evaluate the following types of evidence for the validity of the Christian faith and the divine authorship of the Bible.

experiential evidence:
the unity of the Bible:
the accuracy of the Bible:

prophecy and miracles:
the testimony of Jesus Christ:

Digging Deeper

1. Imagine that you have just received a letter from one of your "party-hardy" buddies from college. Someone told her that you have become a Christian, and she is completely astounded by the news. The last line of her letter says, "Please write soon and tell me it isn't so! Or if it is so, tell me how you could do such a thing!" Write a letter answering her questions and encouraging her to investigate the evidence for Christianity.

2. How would you respond to someone who told you the Bible is not trustworthy because it was put together by a church committee. Research your answer thoroughly by consulting Scripture, church history, and reliable, knowledgeable people.

3

The Right Stuff

The Scriptures are indeed perfect since they were spoken by the Word of God and His Spirit.　　　　　　　—Irenaus

The Word of God is greater than heaven and earth, yea, greater than death and hell, for it forms part of the power of God, and endures everlastingly.　　　　　　　—Martin Luther

We owe to the Scripture the same reverence as we owe to God, since it has its only source in him and nothing of human origin mixed with it.　　　　　　　—John Calvin

The Bible is without mistake because it is God's inspired Word and . . . God cannot lie or contradict Himself.
　　　　　　　—Francis Schaeffer

Several years ago, a popular movie portrayed the uncommon character of the men who pioneered America's space program. The movie highlighted the fact that our first astronauts had a lot more going for them than excellent training. They also had "the right stuff"—a rare combination of personality traits that uniquely suited them for a very demanding job. No amount of determination or knowledge could compensate for lacking "the right stuff"; men without it inevitably washed out of the rigorous training program and never saw the inside of a space capsule.

As we now turn our attention to the uncommon character of the Bible, we will see that it also has "the right stuff" to do a job infinitely more demanding than the work of the space program. The Bible alone, of all the books in the world, is uniquely suited to communicate God's absolute truth to His people. To accomplish that task, the Bible needed an Author possessing insight into and understanding of the mind of God—and only the Holy Spirit qualified (1 Corinthians 2:11). Many books written by human authors have presumptuously declared themselves equal to the task, only to wash out when put to the test.

The Bible has two readily apparent qualities that set it apart from every other book and reflect its perfect ability to communicate God's truth. First of all, it speaks with absolute *authority.* Boldly proclaiming its declarations to be final and binding for all time, it disallows the possibility of correction or revision. Second, the Bible claims compete and total *sufficiency* in the areas of faith and practice that encompass the whole of human life. It tells us that we do not need input from any other source to live in a manner that pleases God.

In this lesson, we will look at the authority of the Bible, and in lesson 4 we will examine its sufficiency.

On Whose Authority?

I love hanging out in card shops—so much so, in fact, that every time my daughter and I pass the Hallmark store in the mall, she grabs my arm and snarls, "Forget it, Mom!" She knows from personal experience just how much time I can spend in front of a display rack reading one greeting card after another.

Being a "word person," I truly appreciate the skill involved in conveying the most complex human thoughts and emotions in a deceptively simple format. Some of the most creative cards I have seen are patterned after official documents, such as diplomas, driver licenses, or traffic tickets. One of my personal favorites is a birthday party invitation designed to look like a jury summons.

Even though these facsimile cards bear a striking resemblance to "the real thing," I have never known anyone to mistake them for the actual document. A greeting card, after all, lacks the *authority* attaching to the real thing. A "jury summons" signed and sealed by my best friend inviting me to appear at her birthday party does not convey the same sense of obligation as does a similar document signed and sealed by the County Clerk "inviting" me to appear at the court house. Obviously, the obligation to comply with the "invitation" derives not from its appearance but from the authority of the person who issued it.

The concept of authority has to do with the right to rule. It involves a *relationship* in which a dominate person (or entity, such as the government) exercises the right to issue directives to and expect compliance from a subordinate person or entity. Therefore, when we say the Bible is *authoritative,* we are alluding to the relationship that exists between its Author and its readers.

God is, of course, the dominant person in the relationship. He is the sovereign, all-powerful, all-knowing, all-controlling Creator and Sustainer of the universe, intimately involved in the continual functioning of every element in that universe. J. I. Packer says, "He, God transcendent, above and beyond and apart from His world, and entirely independent of it, is also God immanent, in the world as the One who is over it, permeating and upholding it as the One who orders its goings and controls its course."[1] When God speaks to us in Scripture, He exercises His right to issue directives and expect compliance (Acts 17:24–31).

Created human beings are innately *subordinate* to His power and control. We are dependent upon Him for every breath, every thought, and every action. Given our utter subjugation to our Creator, attending to His directives constitutes the greater part of wisdom, while disregarding them smacks of foolishness.

Christian faith involves responding submissively to God's rightful authority over us by obeying His written Word. The authority of the *Word* derives from the authority of God's *words*. What the Bible says, God says. The only means of rightly relating to God is by rightly relating to the Incarnate Word as revealed in His written Word. We must *receive* it as the complete presentation of His message (Jude 3), *honor* it as His chosen vehicle of communication (Psalm 138:2), *study* it so as to understand it (2 Timothy 2:15), and *accept* it by conforming our attitudes, thoughts, and behavior to it (Psalm 119:9–11).

Revealed by Inspiration for Illumination

Three key processes are involved in the authoritative communication of God's absolute truth to His people: revelation, inspiration, and illumination. These processes operate solely under the sovereign control of God and, thereby, guarantee preservation of Scripture's authority during its transmission from God to humanity. The first process has to do with Scripture's message, the second with its recording, and the third with its comprehension.

The term *revelation* has to do with disclosure of something that has been concealed. When private investigator Hercule Poirot calls everyone together in the drawing room, you know he is about to reveal the identity of the murderer. Agatha Christie's skillful weaving of clues throughout her stories intentionally gives the reader some hints as to who perpetrated the crime, but if you are anything like me, you frequently misread those clues and zero in on the wrong person. You never know for sure who "done it" until the master detective unmasks the killer in the final scene.

God's revelation works much the same way. He leaves us clues to His identity in nature by means of *natural revelation*. God skillfully weaves these clues throughout His created order to disclose His existence and His power to us, but we frequently misread them.

Psalm 19:1 describes how the "heavens are telling of the glory of God; and their expanse is declaring the work of His hands." Romans 1:20 describes the way God's "invisible attributes, His eternal power and divine nature, have been clearly seen" since the creation of the world, and that these attributes of God can be understood through the things God made. However, Romans 1 also tells us how the human race, through futile speculation and darkened reasoning, misreads these clues and exchanges "the glory of the incorruptible God for an image in the form of corruptible man and of birds and four-footed animals and crawling creatures" (vv. 21–23).

Despite the many clues for the existence of a powerful God in the universe, no one can come to a fuller, saving knowledge of Him through natural revelation alone. Every once in a while, I manage to put Agatha Christie's clues together well enough to identify the murderer, but I always seem to need Hercule to explain how he (or she) did it! Natural revelation tells us that God exists and that He is powerful, but it tells us nothing about how He works. If we are to understand Him more fully, we need more information. And He has graciously given it to us—in the form of *special revelation*.

Special revelation records God's verbal statement of His truth in the Bible. Everything we need to form an understanding of Him, ourselves, and our relationship with Him is written there. God had to *reveal* the message of the Bible to us because we are unable to discover it for ourselves. God explains to us in His Word why this is so.

The Bible describes the way God created humanity in His image as rational beings capable of responding to His commands with freedom of choice. Adam and Eve exercised that freedom by choosing to disobey Him and plunged the human race into total depravity. Our disobedience permeates every aspect of our nature with unrighteousness, warping our understanding of God and eliminating all desire to know Him (Romans 3:10–11). In our depraved condition, we were cut off from God, unable and unwilling to find our way back. Any attempt at reconciliation had to come from Him.

Even though God was under no obligation to pursue reconciliation, His loving nature motivated Him to do so. In order to accomplish this divine purpose, He superintended the writing of a Book detailing the bleakness of our plight and the perfection of His solution. He used human authors to pen this Book, controlling their writing through the process of *inspiration*.

Benjamin B. Warfield describes the inspiration of Scripture as the supernatural influence of God's Holy Spirit exerted on the individual human writers in such a way as to insure the divine trustworthiness of their efforts.[2] The apostle Peter, one of these divinely influenced writers, explains it this way: "But know this first of all, that no prophecy of Scripture is a matter of one's own interpretation, for no prophecy was ever made by an act of human will, but men moved by the Holy Spirit spoke from God" (2 Peter 1:20–21).

In other words, the human authors of God's special revelation used their own words to express God's thoughts precisely the way *He* wanted them expressed. God sovereignly shaped their personalities and their thinking for His own purposes and then supervised their work through the power of the Holy Spirit. Second Timothy 3:16 describes Scripture as being "God-breathed" (NIV). This phrase is built on a Greek verb literally meaning "blow" or "breath out." Therefore, we must not look at Scripture as a human product "breathed into" by the Holy Spirit, but as a Divine product breathed out of God's own Being through the instrumentality of sovereignly controlled men.[3]

Just as the Holy Spirit's work was essential to the writing of Scripture, it is also essential to our comprehending it. This aspect of the Holy Spirit's work is called *illumination.* The Bible was written to teach God's people His truth (John 20:31; Romans 15:4; 1 John 5:13) and cannot be rightly understood without enlightenment from God Himself in the person of His Holy Spirit (1 Corinthians 2:12). This is just one of the many critical ministries of the Holy Spirit that we will examine more closely in lesson 5.

Perfect in Every Way

The sovereign processes controlling both the recording and the comprehension of God's special revelation not only guarantee its absolute authority over our lives, but also guarantee its perfection in every way. A document revealed to us from the mind of God Himself through the process of divine inspiration and understood by supernaturally illumined insight can be nothing less than *infallible* and *inerrant.*

Infallibility refers to the Bible's *inherent* perfection, while *inerrancy* describes its *practical* perfection. Inerrancy flows from infallibility although the reverse is not necessarily true. The fact that my daughter makes 100 percent on a weekly spelling test does not mean that she is incapable of spelling a word wrong. It just means that on this particular test, she knew how to spell all the words. Next week the results may be entirely different! My daughter is an occasionally inerrant speller, but hardly an infallible one.

God, however, *is* infallible. He is incapable of error because He is the very embodiment of truth. The truthfulness of His statements is not measured against some standard outside of Himself. Rather, the truthfulness of all other statements is measured by His declarations. John 17:17 tells us that God's Word is truth, and Psalm 119:160 says, "The sum of Thy Word is truth, and every one of Thy righteous ordinances is everlasting."

The inerrancy of God's Word flows from His infallibility as the sovereign God of the universe. It cannot be otherwise. If the Bible were found to be in error, we would lose more than our confidence in it; we would also lose confidence in our God.

Defying Authority

Many attempts have been and are still being made to shake our confidence in the Bible and in the God who wrote it. The very first attempt was made by the Serpent in the Garden of Eden when he encouraged the woman to question the motives behind God's commands (Genesis 3:1–7). Soon thereafter, Cain superseded God's prescription for sacrificial worship with his own "better idea," and humanity has been following in his footsteps ever since. The children of Israel constantly flirted with the paganism of the world around them, and their leaders elevated their own traditions above the recorded Word of God. Down through the centuries, men and women have continued to exalt their own reasoning above the mind of God, blatantly ignoring the affirmations of Jesus Christ and His chosen apostles concerning the exclusive authority of Scripture (Matthew 4:4; 13:1–23; John 5:24; 8:31; 14:21; 17:14–17; Romans 3:4; Galatians 3:1–3, 21–24; Ephesians 4:11–16; Philippians 3:16; Colossians 3:16; 2 Timothy 4:2; Hebrews 4:12; 2 Peter 2:21; 1 John 2:3).

Some of the most common ways we see this happening today include: (1) limiting the inspiration of the Bible to its *concepts* (but not its actual words) or to certain areas (matters of faith only), (2) restricting the application of Scripture's authority to limited areas of life, (3) forcing the Bible's teaching into conformity with human philosophies, (4) insisting upon the supremacy of ongoing personal revelation, and (5) relying upon faulty interpretation derived from poor study practices.

All of these attempts to undermine Scripture's authority in our lives should be seen for exactly what they are: rebellious defiance of God's authority by sinners bent upon exalting themselves above their Creator. In a word, mutiny.

Check Out That View!

The way you view the authority of the Bible determines, for all practical purposes, the course of your life right now and for all eternity. Your understanding of and reaction to the authority of Scripture sets your priorities, develops your attitudes, structures your activities, controls your behavior, and fixes your eternal dwelling place. There is nothing more deserving of your time and attention than a careful consideration of the authority inherent in the Word of God.

The next time you find yourself close to an old cemetery, take the time to stroll through the rows of headstones noting the dates of birth and death inscribed there. It should not take you long to realize that most of the people lying buried at your feet have been dead a lot longer than they were alive. Eternity is a long time. And the way you view the Bible will determine where you spend it.

Notes

1. J. I. Packer, *God Has Spoken* (Grand Rapids: Baker, 1979), 48.

2. Benjamin B. Warfield, *The Inspiration and Authority of the Bible,* ed. Samuel G. Craig (Philadelphia: Presbyterian and Reformed, 1948), 131.

3. Ibid., 133.

Exercises

Review

1. What is authority? To what are we alluding when we say the Bible is authoritative?

2. What do the following verses teach about the way we should relate to God's Word?

   Jude 3:
   Psalm 138:2:
   2 Timothy 2:15:
   Psalm 119:9–11:

3. Distinguish between *revelation, inspiration,* and *illumination.* How does each contribute to preserving the authority of the Bible in its transmission from God to us?

4. Distinguish between *natural revelation* and *special revelation.* What kinds of things can we learn from special revelation that we cannot learn from natural revelation?

5. Define *infallibility* and *inerrancy.* How are they related? On what is our confidence in the Bible's infallibility and inerrancy based?

6. Explain why a person's view of the Bible is so important. Now, describe *your own* view of the Bible.

Application

1. Read the following verses and record what you learn about the authority of God's Word:

   Psalm 119:9–11:
   Psalm 119:160:
   Matthew 13:1–23:
   John 17:14–17:
   Acts 17:24–31:
   1 Corinthians 2:6–16:
   Colossians 3:16:
   2 Timothy 3:14–16:
   Hebrews 4:12:
   2 Peter 1:20–21:

1 John 5:13:

Revelation 22:18–19:

If you have access to an exhaustive concordance, look up other verses that speak about the authority of God's Word and record what you learn from them also. Construct an outline entitled "The Authority of God's Word" you could use to teach your children, your Sunday school class, your next door neighbor, or a new Christian about the authority of the Bible in their lives.

2. List some general ways in which people today defy the authority of the Word of God, and give a specific example of each. Spend some time praying about whether *you* defy the authority of God in any of these ways. Do you need to pluck up, break down, destroy, or overthrow any rebellious practices in regard to the Bible? Ask God to help you search your heart and confess your sin if necessary.

Digging Deeper

1. What does Psalm 19 tell you about God's revelation of His absolute truth to us? Be sure to include what the psalm tells you about the distinction between natural and special revelation and about the purpose of God's revelation.

2. Throughout history, Christians have acknowledged the authority of tradition, the church, councils, and creeds in establishing their standards of belief and practice. Is this acknowledgment inconsistent with relying on the authority of the Bible as the sole source of absolute truth? Explain your answer thoroughly.

3. Many people agree that the original writings of the Bible were inspired by God and are therefore infallible and authoritative, but they argue that the translations we use today cannot be considered equally reliable. Research the historical processes that preserved the Bible from original autographs to modern

translations and write a brief answer to those who hold such views.

4. Study Psalm 119 (all 176 verses) and prepare a discipling tool of some kind (lesson plan, chart, outline, etc.) that you could use to help a new believer understand the significance of Scripture in her daily walk with the Lord.

4

Enough Is Enough

For indeed the holy and God-breathed Scriptures are self-sufficient for the preaching of the truth. —Athanasius

Where imprecise doctrine and careless biblical exegesis are tolerated, people always tend to look for more than the simple sufficiency God has provided in Christ.
—John MacArthur, Jr.

One of my favorite Bible teachers is a man well known in the Christian community for his unswerving commitment to the authority and sufficiency of Scripture. His convictions so permeate his daily life that on one occasion when he failed to keep a scheduled appointment, the man waiting for him supposedly quipped, "He probably can't find a verse telling him how to get here."

Frankly, I believe we could use more men and women whose convictions speak so loudly in the routine matters of life. Modern Christians, for the most part, have shirked their biblical mandate to stand apart from the world in holiness and allow their righteous distinctiveness to testify of God's greatness (Leviticus 20:26; Numbers 23:9; Deuteronomy 4:20; 1 Peter 2:9). As a matter of fact, most Christians have allowed the world to squeeze them into its mold to such an extent that the church of Jesus Christ appears little different from the Elks Lodge or the Rotary Club.

The apostle Paul in his letter to the Romans warned against such cultural conformity.

> I urge you therefore, brethren, by the mercies of God, to present your bodies a living and holy sacrifice, acceptable to God, which is your spiritual service of worship. And *do not be conformed to this world,* but be transformed by the renewing of your mind, that you may prove what the will of God is, that which is good and acceptable and perfect. (Romans 12:1–2)

Historically, Christianity has had the greatest impact on the world when it has maintained the greatest distinction from it. We are all aware that the brighter the intensity of a light bulb, the greater the impact it has on a dark room. If we dim the light to make it less offensive to the dark room, it ceases to function for its created purpose—to dispel darkness. Becoming like the darkness makes it impossible to overcome the darkness.

In a similar way, when Christians conform themselves to their culture in the name of compatibility, or relevance, or inoffensiveness, they cease to fulfill their created purpose—to display God's glory through their distinctive character and lifestyle. Christians who become like the world cannot possibly overcome the world.

One of the most distinctive manifestations of Christian character is trusting fully in the sufficiency of God's Word as the only infallible guide for life. Christians who consistently strive to accomplish God's purposes *using God's methods* will shine brightly in a dark world as they reflect the perfection of their Creator through radiant Christian living.

Overcomers Can't Just Cope Any More

One of the words I would like to see excised from every Christian's vocabulary is the little word *cope.* Christians are never described in the Bible as "copers" and are never encouraged to engage in the practice of coping. When you look at the dictionary definition of the word, you will see why. Webster's unabridged dictionary says that to cope is "to struggle or contend, especially on fairly even terms or with some degree of success."[1] That's hardly a picture of the worthy Christian walk!

On the contrary, Scripture describes Christians as "overcomers"—people routinely engaged in the practice of overcoming—a far cry from merely coping. The beloved apostle John marks out those who belong to God as *overcomers* (1 John 4:4; 5:4), and the book of Revelation repeatedly refers to those who will reign eternally with Christ as those "who have overcome" (see 2:7, 11, 17, 26; 3:5, 12, 21; 21:7). Paul tells us that Christians who walk worthy of their high calling in Christ are not "overcome by evil" but "overcome evil with good" (Romans 12:21). And John says that we can recognize mature Christians as those who "have overcome the evil one" (1 John 2:13–14). Notice there is not a "coper" in the bunch!

Overcoming the world is not something the Christian can do on his or her own, however (John 15:5). Nor is it something the believer can learn from the world (Isaiah 30:1–3). There is only one source of overcoming power—and that is Jesus Christ Himself.

When Jesus gathered His disciples in the Upper Room on the eve of His crucifixion to prepare them to face the world without Him, I'm sure they thought, *Man, we can't do this!* And they were right. But Jesus told them not to worry. "These things I have spoken to you," He said in John 16:33, "that in Me you may have peace. In the world you have tribulation, but take courage; I have overcome the world." Those men could face the challenge of becoming overcomers the same way we can today. We exist "in Christ," and our ability to overcome the world rests exclusively in the fact that He has already done so.

Jesus also assured His disciples that He was leaving them a Helper—one who would "glorify Me [Christ]; for He shall take of Mine, and shall disclose it to you" (John 16:14). The Holy Spirit was the Helper who came alongside the disciples and equipped them to overcome the world for the glory of God, and He does the same for us today. By inspiring the writing of Scripture and illumining our understanding of it, He equips us to be overcomers as well.

Everything we need to glorify God through the radiant lifestyle of an overcomer is in the Book. We don't need to incorporate worldly techniques and methods into our faith or seek out secular counselors to advise us. One of the greatest overcomers of them all, the apostle Paul, tells us that "God is able to make all grace abound to you, that always having all sufficiency in everything, you may have an abundance for every good deed" (2 Corinthians 9:8), and that we can do all things through Christ who strengthens us (Philippians 4:13).

Scripture itself, as the authoritative Word of God, speaks clearly of its own sufficiency for Christian living. Let's take a look at what it says.

On Good Authority

In a particularly effective series of television commercials, noisy groups of people fell suddenly silent when a certain brokerage firm "spoke." The well-produced spots left the unmistakable impression that this firm knew what it was talking about. Wise investors took its pronouncements on good authority, acted on them, and expected good results.

The things we have learned so far about the Bible assure us that it is much more than a "good authority"—it is the very best authority. Wise Christians listen carefully when Scripture speaks, act on what they hear, and expect perfect results. The inspired writers of Scripture knew what they were talking about. The information they recorded is perfect and entirely sufficient to guide us in the most important job in the world—reflecting God's glory in all the vicissitudes of life.

The apostle Peter, in his second letter, speaks on God's own authority to a group of Christians who were in sore need of encouragement as they faced grievous trials. He reminded them of the *sufficiency of their faith* for enabling them to walk worthy of their high calling in Christ, even in the most difficult circumstances.

> His divine power has granted to us everything pertaining to life and godliness, through the true knowledge of Him

who called us by His own glory and excellence. For by these He has granted to us His precious and magnificent promises, in order that by them you might become partakers of the divine nature, having escaped the corruption that is in the world by lust. (2 Peter 1:3-4)

Three key aspects of the character of Scripture's sufficiency are spelled out in these words of encouragement. Scripture's sufficiency is characterized, first of all, by God's *power*. It's as if Peter tells them, "Remember God's power!" The same God who created the Universe with a word, the same God who raised Christ from the dead with a thought, and the same God who saved them in spite of their utter depravity—this same God had granted them everything they needed for life and godliness. Not some things, not most things, but everything. Christians have what they need in God's Word to overcome anything the world throws at them because His power works through His Word.

The second aspect of Scripture's sufficiency deals with its ability to equip believers to appropriate God's power in daily life. Transferring divine power from the printed page to the real world comes through the *true knowledge of Him* who called us by His own glory and excellence. Living as an overcomer in the sufficiency of spiritual resources requires knowing God well enough to trust His sovereignly ordained purposes for our circumstances.[2]

Scripture's sufficiency becomes increasingly relevant as we learn to shift our focus from self to God. When our lives cease revolving around ourselves and begin revolving around Him (Romans 14:7-8), we see more clearly how Scripture was uniquely designed to equip overcomers to do God's work God's way. If we find Scripture insufficient to accomplish our purposes, we can be sure our purposes are out of harmony with God's (Colossians 3:1-3).

The third aspect of Scripture's sufficiency has to do with God's *promises*. The reason we can confidently place ourselves at His disposal to do His work His way is because of the precious and magnificent promises He has made to us. He has promised to save us and give us eternal life. And He sealed that promise by raising Christ from the dead and giving us the Holy Spirit as a "down payment"

(Romans 4:23–25; Ephesians 1:13–14). He has also promised that He would require nothing of us we cannot handle in His strength and that He would never leave us or forsake us (1 Corinthians 10:13; Hebrews 13:5). Tightening our grip on these promises allows us confidently to say with the writer of Hebrews, "The Lord is my helper, I will not be afraid. What shall man do to me?" (Hebrews 13:6), and with Paul, "If God is for us, who is against us?" (Romans 8:31).

God's promises to His elect people reflect their privileged position as partakers of the divine nature. We partake of God's nature, not as divine beings ourselves, but as beneficiaries of all that He is. Having access to fully sufficient divine resources, we escape "the corruption that is in the world by lust"—in short, we live as overcomers.

These three aspects of Scripture's sufficiency characterize it not as "a compendium of minute details or exhaustive applications" but as an entirely reliable inexhaustible source of divinely inspired principles, "which, when properly interpreted, apply to the minute details of life."[3]

The Bible teacher to whom I referred at the beginning of this lesson may not have been able to find a verse telling him how to get to his appointment, but he did find (and apply) all the biblical principles he needed to help him decide whether to make the appointment in the first place, to order his priorities and give himself time to attend, and to prompt his courteous call to apologize and explain his absence. In short, he found Scripture entirely sufficient to guide his thinking and behavior even in this simple matter.

All Profit, No Loss

The more practical aspects of Scripture's sufficiency are addressed by the apostle Paul in his second letter to his protégé and successor in ministry, Timothy. This particular letter was written to encourage the younger man as he faced the daunting task of stepping into Paul's very large shoes. Second Timothy stresses the *functional* centrality of Scripture's sufficiency in Christian service.

In chapter 3, verses 14–17, Paul says,

You, however, continue in the things you have learned and become convinced of, knowing from whom you have learned them; and that from childhood you have known the sacred writings which are able to give you the wisdom that leads to salvation through faith which is in Christ Jesus. All Scripture is inspired by God and profitable for teaching, for reproof, for correction, for training in righteousness; that the man of God may be adequate, equipped for every good work.

Paul's words emphasize not only Scripture's unique ability to lead us to salvation, but also its unrivaled usefulness as a guide for kingdom service. Scripture's usefulness (its profitability) derives from its inspiration. As we saw in lesson 3, the word translated "inspired" is *theopneustos* in the Greek and literally means "God-breathed." The idea conveyed here is that God actually breathed out the words of Scripture through the Holy Spirit's influence on the human writers.

That "inspiration" was not one of stimulating the human writers to great heights of creative expression, but of moving them to record God's words to humanity (2 Peter 1:20–21). God breathed out Scripture through these writers for a specific purpose: to communicate to us His truths concerning our relationship with Him. He wasted no words. Everything in Scripture serves the purpose for which it was written. It is all profit, no loss.

In verses 16–17, Paul emphasizes four uses of Scripture that, taken together, circumscribe every conceivable aspect of Christian living.

Teaching. Scripture teaches us the truths of God that enable us to understand the significance of our relationship with Him and the importance of living worthy of our high calling in Christ. The didactic portions of Scripture support and give meaning to the imperative portions; we can't *do* what we don't *know*.

Reproof. Scripture also reproves us. The idea behind reproof is rebuke associated with a legal conviction. Scripture judges the thoughts and intentions of our hearts, lays bare every nook and cranny of our souls, and declares us "guilty as charged" of sin against God (Hebrews 4:12). This function of Scripture is absolutely necessary because our natural depravity prevents us from examining ourselves objectively. In Psalm 139, David acknowledged his inability to recognize his own sinfulness and asked God to reveal his need for confession and repentance. "Search me, O God, and know my heart; try me and know my anxious thoughts; and see if there be any hurtful way in me, and lead me in the everlasting way" (vv. 23–24).

Correction. If Scripture's usefulness stopped with reproof, Christianity would be a very depressing venture indeed! But, providentially, it does not. Scripture moves quickly from reproof to correction. Recognition of sin should immediately spur us to appropriate God's corrective measures. The joy that fuels effective Christian witness springs from God's assurance of forgiveness and cleansing when we repent and confess our sin (1 John 1:9).

Satan knows if he can destroy our joy, he can disrupt our effectiveness in God's service by discrediting our testimony. One of the more creative ways he does that is by encouraging us to wallow in the unappealing throes of morbid introspection. No one is drawn to a "god" who fosters misery. Therefore, we must guard against reflecting the true God in such a poor light. Martyn Lloyd-Jones expressed it this way: "Unhappy Christians are, to say the least, a poor recommendation for the Christian Faith; and there can be little doubt but that the exuberant joy of the early Christians was one of the most potent factors in the spread of Christianity."[4]

Training in Righteousness. Scripture's practicality is highlighted by the fact that it moves beyond teaching, reproof, and correction to training in righteousness. In addition to acquainting us with God's truth, pinpointing our sinful failures, and outlining corrective measures, the Bible also trains us in skills of righteous implementation.

Whenever I have the privilege of counseling believers, we usually spend most of our time working in this area. Most Christians who come to me with problems know a great deal of God's truth.

Many of them are sensitive to Scripture's convicting power in their lives. Some even know *what* they need to do in their particular situation. But very few know *how* to do it.

They find themselves in situations similar to the obese woman who *knew* the health ramifications of being overweight, was aware that *she was indeed* too heavy, and *understood* that the only way to lose weight successfully was through diet and exercise. However, she had no idea *how* to eat properly or *how* to begin and maintain a safe exercise program. Without the proper implementation skills, she could not accomplish what she needed *and wanted* to do.

Scripture doesn't drop the ball in our court and wish us Godspeed. It follows through. By providing us a complete package of teaching, reproof, correction, and training in righteousness, it fully equips us for every good work.

The good work that Paul mentions here is undoubtedly a reference to the good works prepared for us before the foundation of the world (Ephesians 2:8–10). The innate character and useful practicality of Scripture's sufficiency is absolutely essential in accomplishing those good works to the glory of God. When we ignore it or dilute it with worldly additives, we short-circuit God's perfect means of doing His work His way, and rob Him of glory and ourselves of joy (Isaiah 30:1–3; Jeremiah 2:18–19; Colossians 2:6–10).

Notes

1. *Webster's Encyclopedic Unabridged Dictionary of the English Language* (Avenal, N.J.: Random House Value, 1989).

2. For a detailed treatment of this subject, see the author's study, *James on Trials* (Los Alamos, N.M.: Deo Volente, forthcoming).

3. David G. Hagopian, ed., *Back to Basics: Rediscovering the Richness of the Reformed Faith* (Phillipsburg, N.J.: P&R Publishing, 1996), 282.

4. D. Martyn Lloyd-Jones, *Spiritual Depression: Its Causes and Cure* (Grand Rapids: Eerdmans, 1965), foreword.

Exercises

Review

1. Read Leviticus 20:26, Numbers 23:9, Deuteronomy 4:20, 1 Peter 2:9, and Romans 12:1–2, and explain why Christians should not conform to the world. How does understanding and relying upon the sufficiency of Scripture help us refrain from conforming to the world?

2. Describe an overcomer. How does an overcomer differ from a coper?

3. List three key aspects of the *character* of Scripture's sufficiency found in 2 Peter 1:3–4. How does each of these aspects contribute to living as an overcomer in the world?

4. List four practical aspects of Scripture's sufficiency found in 2 Timothy 3:16–17. How does each of these aspects contribute to living as an overcomer in the world?

5. Explain why the innate character and practical usefulness of Scripture's sufficiency is essential in accomplishing the good works God prepared for us to do before the world began.

6. What does inspiration have to do with the sufficiency of Scripture?

Application

1. Describe a time when your faith in Christ allowed (or required) you to stand distinctly separate from the world. (Describe the situation you were in and what you did that set you apart from those around you.)

   What kind of impact did your distinctiveness have on those around you?

   What part did Scripture play in this situation? (Did it convict you about the need the take a stand, show you how to be distinct, encourage you in persecution, etc.? Give specific verses.)

What did you learn about the sufficiency of Scripture from this situation? Would you respond any differently to the same situation today?

2. If you had a difficult time doing "Application" 1, reread Leviticus 20:26, Numbers 23:9, Deuteronomy 4:20, 1 Peter 2:9, and Romans 12:1–2. Pray over and meditate on these verses, asking the Lord to reveal whether you are living a life of holy distinction. As He begins to answer your prayers, record any specific areas of your life that need to become more distinctly Christian, and make a detailed plan to make the necessary changes. Share your plan with someone who loves you enough to hold you accountable for following through on your intentions.

3. Describe an area of your life in which you would like to become more Christlike. (If you can't think of any, try humility.) Using 2 Timothy 3:16–17 as a guide and an exhaustive concordance as a tool, list verses of Scripture that (1) teach you God's truth about this area of life, (2) reprove you by telling you how you have failed in this area, (3) correct you by telling you how you need to think and act in this area, and (4) provide you with training to become more Christlike in this area. (For example, if you want to become more Christlike in your speech, you might select Colossians 4:5–6 as a teaching passage, James 3:6 as a reproof passage, Colossians 3:16–17 as a correction passage, and Ephesians 4:25–29 as training verses.) Give *specific examples* of how each passage of Scripture applies to your particular situation. Then evaluate the sufficiency of Scripture to promote Christlikeness in this area.

Digging Deeper

1. Research secular self-help literature on the subject of "coping" and biblical literature on the subject of "overcoming." Write a character sketch of a coper and an overcomer. In view of the fact that Christians are called to glorify God and enjoy Him forever by walking worthy of their high calling in Christ, explain

why the Bible always describes Christians as *overcomers* and not as *copers*. How might this study equip you to minister to someone who is experiencing difficult problems?

2. Defend the sufficiency of Scripture to someone who says to you, "Since the Bible contains only a few verses that refer specifically to raising children, it is simply not sufficient to meet all my needs as a parent in our day and age. In order to raise my children well, I must supplement Scripture with the advice of secular experts."

5

The Illuminator

*The Holy Spirit may be distinguished from the Word, but to sep-
arate the Word and the Spirit is spiritually fatal. The Holy Spirit
teaches, leads and speaks to us through the Word and with the
Word, not apart from or against the Word.*

—R. C. Sproul

*Ignorance of the third Person of the Godhead is most dishon-
oring to Him and highly injurious to ourselves.*

—A. W. Pink

My daughter was born with beautiful long eyelashes—and a
clogged tear duct in her right eye. Her doctors decided to wait until
she was a year old to surgically open the duct, but changed their
minds when a rapidly spreading infection invaded both of those
little eyes almost three months before the scheduled operation.

While we were waiting for the antibiotics to clear the infection suf-
ficiently for the surgeon to work safely, she would frequently awaken
with both eyes firmly glued shut. The nightly accumulation of sticky
infectious matter encrusted on those beautiful long eyelashes made
it impossible for her to open her eyes without the loving intervention of a concerned mom armed with a warm washcloth.

The Holy Spirit, armed with God's Word, works on our encrusted, sin-infected eyes much as I worked on my daughter's. Without His patient, loving intervention, our eyes remain firmly glued shut to God's absolute truth, and we remain helpless to get them open. God's Holy Spirit is, indeed, the Divine Illuminator, who opens our eyes so that we may behold wonderful things in God's law (Psalm 119:18).

The Holy Spirit bears full responsibility for carrying out God's plan of communicating His truth to His people by illuminating an inspired revelation to the understanding of the elect. His work is extremely important, and extremely unusual, particularly in our self-absorbed age, for He works without calling any attention to Himself.

No Footprints in the Sand

The way the Holy Spirit works can be likened to the efforts of a skilled editor. The best editors labor invisibly, focusing all their creative energy on perfecting *someone else's* work. The less evident their involvement, the more effectively they work.

Abraham Kuyper captured this element of the Holy Spirit's character when he said, "The Holy Spirit leaves no footprints in the sand."[1] John MacArthur expressed it in the title of a book about Him, *The Silent Shepherd.*[2] And my own pastor, Randy Steele, alluded to it when he taught our Sunday evening study group that the Holy Spirit is the expert "artisan" of the Trinity who devotes Himself to faithfully finishing the work designed by the Father and accomplished by the Son.[3]

These men have accurately portrayed the Spirit's work habits by restating what Jesus taught about Him in John 16:13–15.

> But when He, the Spirit of truth, comes, He will guide you into all the truth; for He will not speak on His own initiative, but whatever He hears, He will speak; and He will disclose to you what is to come. He shall glorify Me; for He shall take of Mine, and shall disclose it to you. All things that the Father has are Mine; therefore I said, that He takes of Mine, and will disclose it to you.

A Two-Part Plan

God's eternal plan for the elect includes two basic elements: *regeneration* and *sanctification.*[4] *Regeneration,* simply put, is the change that occurs in us when we are saved. Before salvation, we are hard-hearted and insensitive to the plans and purposes of God; after salvation, we are soft-hearted and sensitive to Him. Before salvation, we are incapable of understanding and responding to His commands; after salvation, we are able to do both (Ezekiel 11:19–20; 36:25–27). This change occurs instantaneously at the moment we are saved.

Sanctification, on the other hand, is the process of living out that change. It involves responding to our new sensitivity in obedience to God and acting on our new ability for the purpose of glorifying God and enjoying Him forever (John 15:7–11).

Before salvation, our lives revolved around ourselves; after salvation, they revolve around Him.

The participation of each member of the Trinity is essential in carrying out God's plan for the elect. The Father devised the plan, the Son carried out the plan, and the Spirit applies the plan to the elect. The plan involves our participation also. Regeneration stimulates our genuine response of faith to the effectual call of salvation, and sanctification demands our active obedience to God's commands as we work out our salvation according to the power that works within us.

In and Through the Word

The Holy Spirit *applies* God's plan by working in and through the Word of God to enable us to fulfill our participatory responsibilities. Even though our participation is truly *ours,* it is made possible by the Spirit's empowering (Philippians 2:12–13). Without Him, we would not understand God's requirements of us, nor would we be able to do what He requires (John 15:5).

Perhaps the easiest way to see how the Holy Spirit works in and through Scripture to regenerate and sanctify us is to remind ourselves of the innate characteristics and practical uses of Scripture discussed in lesson 4. You will recall that 2 Peter 1:3–4 characterized Scripture as being filled with God's power, able to equip believers for service through a true knowledge of God, and energized by confidence-inspiring promises. Second Timothy 3:16 spelled out Scripture's usefulness in four areas that encompass the whole of the Christian life: teaching, reproof, correction, and training in righteousness. A little further investigation will reveal the Holy Spirit's active involvement in each of these areas also.

The power of God that characterizes Scripture is the power of the Holy Spirit. He is omniscient (1 Corinthians 2:11), omnipresent (Psalm 139:7–10), and omnipotent (Job 33:4). The true knowledge of God contained in the Bible comes by the witness of the Holy Spirit who is identified as truth itself (1 John 5:7). The Holy Spirit is also the seal and guarantor of God's promises recorded in Scripture (2 Corinthians 1:20–22; Galatians 3:14; Ephesians 1:13).

The Holy Spirit *teaches* us by revealing to our regenerated minds the wisdom of God that is completely unintelligible to unregenerated men and women (1 Corinthians 2:6–16). His work is so effective in this area that we are said to "have the mind of Christ." What an awesome statement!

He *reproves* us by convicting us of sin, righteousness, and judgment (John 16:8). The Holy Spirit's work of conviction sets the stage for regeneration by showing us our lost condition and God's gracious provision of salvation (John 3:5–8). The Spirit continues working in our sanctification by sharpening our sensitivity to sin and driving us back to God for His continual cleansing forgiveness (1 John 1:9).

The Holy Spirit *corrects us* by taking the things of Christ and disclosing them to us (John 16:14–15). By exalting Christ's perfect obedience, which secured our salvation, the Spirit sets before us a perfect example of righteousness to emulate (1 Peter 1:13–16; 1 John 2:6).

Finally, the Spirit *trains us in righteousness* through His ongoing work of sanctification (2 Thessalonians 2:13). One of Jesus' primary concerns for His disciples was their sanctification. As He prays for them on the eve of His crucifixion, He asks God to "sanctify them in the truth" and adds a word of commentary, "Thy Word is truth" (John 17:17). The apostle John, who was with Jesus that night and went on to record much of that Word of Truth, equates the work of the Word with the work of the Spirit when He says, "The Spirit is the truth" (1 John 5:7). Scripture thus teaches that training in righteousness (sanctification) occurs through the duel "out-breathings" of God in His Word and in His Spirit.

The work of the Spirit and the work of the Word are truly inseparable. In this age of experience-oriented faith, it is essential to remember that the Spirit of God never leads us apart from, away from, or contrary to the Word of God recorded in Scripture.

A Holy Alliance

Throughout history, alliances have been formed to accomplish goals. Nations ally with one another to make war and then re-ally to keep the peace. Congressional representatives caucus and compromise to assure passage of important legislation. Public interest groups join together to improve the quality of life, and parents seek to present a "united front" in rearing their children. All of these human alliances achieve varying levels of success, depending upon the personal commitment of their members to the individual cause. Wavering commitments often lead to broken alliances.

The alliance of the Word of God with the Spirit of God to regenerate and sanctify the elect, however, cannot fail. It will accomplish what it was created to do. It is, in effect, an alliance of God with Himself. Throughout the Bible, we find references to the Word and the Spirit participating in and accomplishing the same activities, reinforcing for our understanding the inseparable nature of their ministries.

The new life (regeneration) that accompanies salvation is spoken of as a work of the Word in Matthew 4:4 and of the Spirit in Titus 3:5. Acting out that new life in sanctification is also presented as a work of the Word and of the Spirit (John 17:17; 2 Thessalonians 2:13). The Word of God comforts us in time of need (Psalm 119:50) as does His Spirit (John 16:7). Scripture and the Spirit are wise co-counselors who help us understand God's purposes in our lives (Psalm 119:24; John 15:26). They also help us understand ourselves (Hebrews 4:12; 1 Corinthians 2:10–11). They equip us to do the work of God and give us hope for the future (1 Corinthians 2:9–10; 2 Peter 1:3–4; Titus 2:11–15).

Two passages of Scripture connect the work of the Spirit with the work of the Word perhaps more clearly than any others: Ephesians 5:18–6:9 and Colossians 3:16–4:6. A quick overview of these two passages highlights their remarkable similarity. Both refer to addressing one another with psalms, hymns, and spiritual songs that reflect the gratefulness we feel toward God for our salvation. Both then describe a pattern of biblical relationships flowing out of that attitude. Godly husbands, wives, children, employers, and employees see their interpersonal relationships, not as a means of self-exaltation or gratification, but as a means of glorifying God in thankfulness for the rich blessings of eternal life. And both passages end with an all-encompassing admonition to "render service" or to "do your work" as to the Lord and not for men.

The interesting thing about these almost identical passages is that they are describing the results of two different activities. The Ephesians passage concerns "being filled with the Spirit" (5:18), while the Colossians passage speaks to letting "the Word of Christ richly dwell within you" (3:16). This simple observation leads us to the conclusion that being filled with the Spirit produces exactly the same results as does letting the Word richly dwell within you. They produce the same results because they work together—inseparably.

The Plan Summary

Jesus neatly summarized God's plan for redeeming and sanctifying the elect in John 15:16 when He said, "You did not choose Me, but I chose you, and appointed you, that you should go and bear fruit, and that your fruit should remain, that whatever you ask of the Father in My name, He may give to you."

God chose us and appointed us to stand apart from the world in holiness. We are to bear fruit—fruit that remains because it is generated in us by the eternal Spirit of God. That fruit glorifies God because, being produced by Him, it reflects His character and nature. God also planned that we should enjoy an intimate, parent-child relationship with Him in which everything we need to accomplish His work in us would be supplied by Him as we request it. The plan was perfect, and its communication to fallen men and women was also perfect. God revealed His plan to us through the means of His written Word, inspired and illumined by His own Spirit.

When we study and apply Scripture in submission to the Spirit's guiding authority, we fulfill our cherished role in accomplishing His plan. As we grow in a true knowledge of God, we become a people for His own possession, zealous for good deeds and demonstrating the fruit of the Spirit in our daily lives. We walk according to the hope of eternal life, looking for the blessed hope and appearing of the glory of our great God and Savior, Christ Jesus.[5] In short, we carry out our created purpose of glorifying God and enjoying Him forever.

In lesson 6, we will look at some practical ways to begin appropriating scriptural truth in the power of the Holy Spirit.

Notes

1. Cited in R. C. Sproul, *The Mystery of the Holy Spirit* (Wheaton, Ill.: Tyndale House, 1990), 7.

2. John MacArthur, Jr., *The Silent Shepherd* (Wheaton, Ill.: Victor, 1996).

3. Randy L. Steele, "Studies in Genesis" (unpublished study series delivered at Providence Presbyterian Church, Albuquerque, NM, 1997).

4. For an in-depth treatment of these two subjects, see John Murray, *Redemption Accomplished and Applied* (Grand Rapids: Eerdmans, 1955).

5. See 2 Peter 1:3–4; Galatians 5:16–26; Titus 2:11–15; 3:4–7.

Exercises

Review

1. Explain the Holy Spirit's role in communicating God's truth to His people.

2. Define and distinguish between *regeneration* and *sanctification*.

3. What role does each member of the Trinity play in God's plan to redeem and sanctify the elect? What part do we, the elect, play? Support your answer with Scripture.

4. Explain, in your own words, how the work of the Holy Spirit is related to the character and usefulness of Scripture described in 2 Peter 1:3–4 and 2 Timothy 3:16–17. Support your answer with Scripture.

5. Explain how Ephesians 5:18–6:9 and Colossians 3:16–4:6 demonstrate the inseparability of the work of the Word and the work of the Spirit.

6. How does John 15:16 summarize redemption and sanctification? (Be careful not to make this question harder than it is.)

Application

1. Respond biblically to someone who says to you, "I don't need to read or study the Bible because I am mature enough in my faith to listen to the Holy Spirit and follow His direction."

2. Some "Christian counselors" believe the Bible can be used to help unbelievers deal with problems of living. They support their belief by saying that anyone can understand and apply biblical principles, and since they are God's principles for living, they will work. Based upon what you have learned in this lesson about the Holy Spirit's work, explain what is wrong with this reasoning. (Hint: See 1 Corinthians 2:6–16).

   If an unbeliever came to you, a Christian, for "counseling," where would you begin? (Hint: Think about 1 Corinthians 2:6–16. What must occur in a person's life before we can expect him or her to receive and implement the wisdom of God contained in Scripture?)

3. Make a list of each area of life addressed by Ephesians 5:18–6:9 and Colossians 3:16–4:6. Select one or more of these areas in which your own life does not fully glorify God. Pray and ask the Holy Spirit to illumine your understanding of these two passages in relation to your specific situation. Then record the changes you need to make in order to obey God in these areas. How will your obedience glorify God? How will it increase your joy in Him? Try to answer these questions specifically.

4. Are you zealous for good deeds? Do you walk in hope, looking for the blessed hope and appearing of the glory of our great God and Savior, Jesus Christ? Do you bear fruit? Evaluate your life honestly in these areas. (Try asking someone who knows you very well to help you.)

    If you can answer "yes" to these questions, even though you need to improve in all of them, how does this exercise contribute to your assurance of salvation?

Digging Deeper

1. R. C. Sproul says that "to separate the Word and the Spirit is spiritually fatal." And A. W. Pink has said, "Ignorance of the third Person of the Godhead is . . . highly injurious to ourselves." Based on your study of this lesson and any further research you care to do, explain the reasoning behind these two statements in your own words.

2. The well-known literary vignette *Footprints* reads as follows:

    One night a man had a dream. He dreamed he was walking along the beach with the LORD. Across the sky flashed scenes from his life. . . . For each scene he noticed two sets of footprints in the sand, one belonging to him, and one to the LORD.

    When the last scene of his life flashed before him, he looked back at the footprints in the sand. He noticed that many times along the path of his life there was only one set of footprints. He also noticed that it happened at the very lowest and saddest times of his life.

This really bothered him, and he questioned the LORD about it . . . "LORD, you said that once I decided to follow you, you'd walk with me all the way. But I have noticed that during the most troublesome times in my life, there is only one set of footprints. I don't understand why when I needed you most you would leave me."

The LORD replied, "My precious, precious child, I love you and I would never leave you. During your times of trial and suffering when you see only one set of footprints, it was then that I carried you." (Author unknown)

Abraham Kuyper may have had this vignette in mind when he said, "The Holy Spirit leaves no footprints in the sand." Explain, in your own words, what you think Kuyper meant by that statement.

6

What Am I Supposed to Do with This?

Not to know the Scriptures is to be ignorant of Christ.
—St. Jerome

Not only is Scripture the fountainhead for knowledge of God, Christ and salvation, but it presents this knowledge in an incomparably vivid, powerful and evocative way.
—J. I. Packer

And those who have insight will shine brightly like the brightness of the expanse of heaven, and those who lead the many to righteousness like the stars for ever and ever.
—Daniel 12:3

"Guido" was a funny-looking little mutt who stole my heart at a church picnic and quickly became a cherished member of our family. He had inherited such a remarkably incompatible assortment of physical characteristics from his mismatched parents that we affectionately described him as "aesthetically challenged." The one and only time I hopefully presented Guido to a professional groomer for sprucing up, she looked him over carefully and then asked me rather quizzically, "Just what am I supposed to do with him?"

At this point in our study, some of you may be asking yourselves the same question. We have devoted a great deal of time and attention in the last five lessons to examining the Bible carefully, but you may still be unsure of just what you are supposed to do with it. Fortunately, I have an answer for you, even though I didn't have one for my puzzled groomer!

Basically, you are "supposed to do" five things with the Bible: hear it, read it, study it, memorize it, and meditate on it.

Listen, My Children

One of the most vivid lessons I have learned from my involvement in counseling and discipling ministries is that most people don't listen very well. We hear quite a bit. As a matter of fact, we seem to be addicted to noise in our culture. Ask people why the television or the radio or the stereo is on, and they will typically tell you they "have to have" some kind of noise in the background. Absolute silence can be extremely uncomfortable and downright distressing at times.

My daughter and I had this truth brought home to us several years ago. A friend of mine from college invited us to spend the weekend with her in the small, mountain community of Cuba, New Mexico. She tucked us in for the night and wished us a good rest. But it was not to be. We tossed and turned for several hours and finally sat up in bed to gaze through the open window at the peaceful moonlit town scattered below us. "I am so tired," I said. "I don't know why I can't get to sleep." My daughter, with simple twelve-year old wisdom replied, "Mom, it's just too quiet." She was right. We were used to city noise—and so distressed by country quiet that we couldn't sleep.

I recall when waiting to see the doctor, standing in line at the grocery store, and sitting in an airplane terminal were relatively silent experiences. Now, with Muzak and ubiquitous television, they are not. Quiet places are becoming rarer all the time. Interestingly enough, all the exercise our ears are getting doesn't seem to strengthen our ability to listen at all. We hear, but we don't receive. The deluge of sound constantly washing over us numbs our consciousness without penetrating it. Noise interferes with listening because it diffuses our ability to concentrate and distracts us from focusing on any one thing. We hear so much, we don't really *listen* to any of it.

Tragically, hearing without listening affects our relationship with God. We grow so accustomed to mental distraction that even when we find ourselves in a quiet environment conducive to listening, we create distraction to reestablish our comfort zone. How many times have you caught yourself sitting in a quiet church service— where the only sound is the voice of a godly pastor-teacher expounding the Word of God—thinking about your dinner menu or the argument you had with your husband last night? Your environment is not distracting you from listening to what you are hearing; you are, by force of habit, distracting yourself.

When I counsel and disciple other believers, the most difficult task before me, without exception, is listening to what someone is saying and responding accordingly. My natural tendency is to tune her out while I rehearse in my mind the grand presentation of eloquent gems of wisdom I am prepared to give her as soon as she quits talking! That distraction is not coming from my environment either. It's coming from me—fallen, depraved, sinful, prideful me.

When the prophet Amos described a famine "for hearing the words of the LORD" (Amos 8:11), he was referring not so much to a time when the words of the Lord would cease to fall upon our ears as to a time when we would not listen to the words we were hearing. Hearing so as to listen requires effort. It demands concentration and focus. It doesn't happen without discipline and self-control. It forces us to act upon Philippians 2:12–13 by relying upon the indwelling Holy Spirit's power to enable us to work at listening.

When the Bible tells us to "hear" the word of the Lord, it is telling us to listen—to work at comprehension and obedience. Jesus compared the person who "hears these words of Mine, and acts upon them" to "a wise man, who built his house upon the rock." When the storms of life beat upon that house, it stood firm. In the next breath, Jesus compared the person "who hears these words of Mine, and does not act upon them" to "a foolish man, who built his house upon the sand." When the storms of life beat upon his house, "it fell, and great was its fall" (Matthew 7:24–27).

What are you supposed to do with the Bible? First of all, hear it so as to listen to it and practice it. Put yourself in places where it is being read, taught, and preached. Discipline yourself to concentrate on understanding and applying what you are hearing. Hearing the word of God, in the biblical sense, has to do with the kind of active listening that builds faith (Romans 10:17).

Read Any Good Books Lately?

The second thing you are supposed to do with the Bible is read it. As we mentioned in lesson 1 of this study, reading is rapidly becoming a lost art in our culture. As we grow increasingly picture-oriented, our desire to read seems to decrease almost exponentially. When we do read, we look for something *entertaining*—action packed thrillers that immerse us in vicarious excitement or romantic adventures that stir our emotions. Reading for pleasure may still entice a few of us, but reading for thought is just too hard for most of us.

As Christians committed to accomplishing God's purposes rather than our own, we need to overcome our aversion to serious reading. God chose to disclose His revelation in a serious-minded Book because that medium conforms most closely to the nature of His revelation. Neglecting His chosen method of communication amounts to open rebellion against Him. We must see a return to reading the Bible for what it is—obedience to God's commands that may include repentance and confession of sin. We must resist the pull of our culture and not allow the world to squeeze us into its mold. We must realize that the only way we can be transformed by the renewing of our minds is by heeding the message contained in the Book (Romans 12:1–2)—and we usually can't do that without reading it!

We should also be concerned with reading it *well*. It always amazes me when people "read the Bible" in disconnected chunks. They wouldn't dream of reading Tolstoy or Shakespeare or Clancy or Grisham in such a hit or miss fashion. But they seem to think "pick and choose" is a perfectly reasonable approach to reading the Bible. It isn't. The Bible tells one consistent coherent story from start to finish and should be read with the specific intent of understanding its entire message in context. This requires reading whole books (all sixty-six of them) and the whole Book (from start to finish). It requires reading and rereading and rereading and rereading. It requires some serious time and some serious thought to understand the overall message.

This kind of reading provides the necessary contextual framework for concentrated study of specific portions of Scripture because it supports responsible interpretation. Much of the faulty doctrine and misunderstanding of God's truth permeating the church today has resulted from failure to interpret portions of Scripture within the context of the whole counsel of God. And the best way to guard against such "truth abuse" is to read through the Bible regularly.

There are many excellent "Bible reading plans" available today that take you through the Bible in a specific period of time. If you haven't already done so, find one you like and start reading! That is far and away the very best preparation for *studying* the Bible— which is the next thing you should be doing with it.

Hidden Treasure

For many years a big ugly rock lay two-feet deep in a shallow North Carolina brook. People passing by the stream paid little attention to it until one poor but resourceful man recognized its potential as an excellent, and much needed, doorstop for his home. He hauled it out of the stream and, with great satisfaction, put it to good use. A few months later, a trained geologist stopped to visit the poor but resourceful man, took one look at the doorstop, and asked in astonishment, "Why are you using a huge gold nugget for a doorstop!" The nugget was said to be the largest ever found east of the Rockies and was valued by Tiffany's at over $100,000.[1]

That little story aptly illustrates the value of, as well as the distinction between, *reading* and *studying* the Bible. Those who routinely ignore the Bible are like those North Carolinians who walked passed that gold nugget every day with no idea of its real worth. Those who read the Bible are like the poor but resourceful man who did realize some legitimate benefit from his use of the stone. But only those, like the trained geologist, who invest energy and effort in concentrated study will be able to appreciate the full value of what is lying right in front of them.

The book of Proverbs puts it this way:

> Make your ear attentive to wisdom,
> Incline your heart to understanding;
> For if you cry for discernment,
> Lift your voice for understanding;
> If you seek her as silver,
> And search for her as for hidden treasures;
> Then you will discern the fear of the LORD,
> And discover the knowledge of God. (Proverbs 2:2–5)

Even though the blessings and benefits of Scripture *reading* are genuine and useful, the blessings and benefits of Bible *study* multiply at an astounding rate. Bible study reveals the hidden gems of wisdom that lie beneath the surface of superficial reading. Such treasures are surprisingly accessible to all Christians.

Effective Bible study begins with effective reading. Good Bible students are careful *observers.* They read carefully, think critically, and question everything. When they read the Bible, they ask themselves, *What does this passage of Scripture actually say?* To answer that question, they look at context, key words, and manner of presentation. Instead of forcing the passage to say what they want it to say, they work at understanding what the author meant when he wrote these words.

When a good Bible student is satisfied that she knows what the passage says, she then asks, *What does it mean?* Answering this question takes her into the realm of interpretation—an area that requires humble submission to the Holy Spirit and some basic training in sound study techniques. Responsible interpretation begins with identifying an author's purpose for writing and the fundamental themes he uses to achieve his purpose. That purpose and those themes then need to be fitted into God's overall revelation and understood within the appropriate historical and grammatical context.

In the May/June 1996 issue of *Modern Reformation* magazine, V. Philips Long described the Bible as "literary theological history."[2] Interpreting literary theological history responsibly requires familiarity with literary devices, theological concepts, and historical facts. And that nearly always requires a certain amount of training to supplement a humble attitude. If you have never learned how to study the Bible as literary theological history, make it a point to do so as soon as possible. Another book in this series, *Turning On the Light,* might be a good place to start.

Good Bible students also ask one last question before they consider their study complete, and that is *How does this apply to me?* Effective Bible study always culminates in application, but it can't begin there. Before you can apply the wisdom contained in the passage you are studying, you must understand what it says as well as what it means.

Study is hard work, but well worth the effort. You can keep using that $100,000 nugget for a doorstop if you like, but I can't imagine why you'd want to!

You Got a Verse for That?

One of my best friends constantly challenges me to think biblically. She often responds to my opinionated comments with, "You got a verse for that?" She has been, without a doubt, a very good influence on my thinking, as well as on my attitude toward Scripture memory.

For a large part of my Christian life, I was not convinced that memorizing Scripture was a worthwhile use of my time. But then my friend came along with her persistent little question and gave me at least one good reason to get started. Not long afterward, the Lord began to show me several much better reasons to memorize His Word.

First of all, it keeps us from sinning against God. Psalm 119:11 says, "Thy Word I have treasured in my heart, that I may not sin against Thee." When we store Scripture in the recesses of our hearts, conviction strikes swift and sure. I can't count the number of times an "unwholesome word" has left my brain only to be turned back at my teeth by Ephesians 4:29 standing guard over my mouth.

Scripture memory also gives us immediate guidance in the routine decisions of life (Psalm 119:105), courage for service (1 Corinthians 15:58), confidence in persecution (Psalm 118:6–9), purpose for living (Ephesians 2:8–10), and hope for the future (1 John 3:1–3). The key word in the previous sentence is "immediate." Christians who memorize Scripture don't have to dig out their concordances and conduct a word search every time they have a need. Getting the Word off the page and into your mind allows the Holy Spirit to minister to you when you need it most—immediately.

Most of us are far more easily convinced that we should memorize Scripture than we are that we can actually do it. Whenever someone says to me, "I just can't memorize anything," I like to respond with "What about your phone number? What about your children's birthdays? What about 'Two all beef patties, special sauce, lettuce, cheese, pickles, onions on a sesame-seed bun'?" Almost everyone can and does memorize lots of things!

Memorization involves transferring information from short-term storage to long-term storage in the brain. There are many ways to do that. The trick is finding a way that works for you. Some people like to record verses on tape and listen to them over and over in the car. Some people write verses on cards and carry them around to read and repeat during typically "dead" periods of time—waiting in lines, sitting at stop lights, etc. Some people memorize short phrases and build up to an entire verse. Others find it easier to memorize the whole verse as a chunk. Some people like to work with a partner, and some like to work alone.

There is no "right way" to memorize Scripture. Try several methods until you find the one that best suits your personality and lifestyle. And don't get discouraged when you think the process is taking too long. Even if it takes you a month to learn one verse, at the end of the year, you will have a dozen gems of wisdom stored in your mental vault available for immediate use by the Holy Spirit in your sanctification.[3]

Lost Words

It is truly unfortunate that so many good words have been so tainted by worldly connotations that Christians hesitate to use them. I seldom use the words *gay, evolve,* and *visualize* unless I am referring to the worldly concept with which they have become associated. However, I refuse to give up the word *meditate* even though it, too, is developing a distinctly New Age flavor.

Meditation, the fifth thing you should be doing with the Scripture, is the key ingredient in walking worthy of your high calling in Christ. Meditation is activated by consistently hearing, reading, studying, and memorizing the Word of God. For the Christian, it is not some mystical ritual involving mantras, gurus, and incense. It is the process of carrying Scripture around in your mind and thinking about it—either directly or indirectly.

Paul alludes to meditation when he says, "Let the word of Christ richly dwell within you" (Colossians 3:16). The word *dwell* in this context has to do with settling down and being at home. It happens when your thinking is so saturated with Scripture that you begin to respond instinctively (another word many Christians hesitate to use) to situations of life righteously rather than sinfully. When your mind is filled with Scripture, your behavior is much easier to control. David saw this connection when he prayed, "Let the words of my mouth and the meditation of my heart be acceptable in Thy sight, O Lord, my rock and my Redeemer" (Psalm 19:14).

What kinds of things do you carry around in your mind? Where do your thoughts tend to wander? If your daydreams were made into a movie, would you allow your children to see it? The answers to these questions describe the meditation of your heart—and reveal how effectively you are hearing, reading, studying, and memorizing the Word of God.

Make a Plan

Someone has wisely said, "When you fail to plan, you plan to fail." The apostle James put it this way, "Prove yourselves doers of the word, and not merely hearers who delude themselves" (James 1:22). The point of both statements is this: Knowing what you are supposed to do with the Bible is not enough. You must actually do it. And that requires some planning. Begin today thinking about practical ways you can hear, read, study, memorize, and meditate on Scripture so that you can more effectively carry out your created purpose of glorifying God and enjoying Him forever.

Unified—in Wisdom—for Service

The president of the Women in the Church (WIC) council of the church I attend in Albuquerque is emphasizing "unity and wisdom" in all of this year's WIC activities. As a dedicated Christian leader in the church, she understands the destructiveness of disunity within the body of Christ. And as a mature Christian woman, she also understands the secret of maintaining the kind of unity that glorifies God and benefits us. True Christian unity comes only through appropriating the wisdom of God contained in the Bible, which equips us to fulfill our created purpose of serving our King.

The transforming power of salvation revealed in God's Word draws us together as we strive toward our shared goal of conformity to Christ. The closer each of us draws to Him, the closer we draw to each other. United in spirit by the Holy Spirit, we close ranks around one common purpose—that of testifying of God's glory and grace to a lost and dying world (Philippians 2:2). We do this because God is answering the prayer of His Son that we would all be one even as He and the Father are One, so that the world would know the truth about His incarnation (John 17:21).

God assures us in Isaiah 46:10 that He will establish His purposes and accomplish all His good pleasure. Answering His Son's prayer for the elect is certainly included in His purposes and good pleasure. Satan knows he cannot thwart God's ultimate plans for the universe, but he hates Him enough to do all in his power to disrupt the powerful testimony of God's elect. One of his most successful tactics is divisiveness. The apostle James provides wise counsel regarding how we must deal with the Enemy's tactics. "Submit therefore to God. Resist the devil and he will flee from you. Draw near to God and He will draw near to you" (James 4:7–8).

Resisting Satan involves submitting to God by drawing near to Him—and our only means of doing that is through His Word in the power of His Spirit. When we join our hearts and minds with those of our brothers and sisters in Christ around God's revealed Truth, we magnify our effectiveness, intensify our witness, and heighten our joy.

As you complete this study, spend some time in prayer asking your Father to deepen your commitment to hearing, reading, studying, memorizing, and meditating upon His absolute truth revealed in the Bible, so that you can become thoroughly equipped to fulfill your essential role in unifying the body of Christ in wisdom for service.

Notes

1. Adapted from Paul Lee Tan, *Encyclopedia of 7,700 Illustrations: Signs of the Times* (Rockville, Md.: Assurance, 1979), 953.

2. V. Philips Long, "What Does the Bible Tell Me About History?" *Modern Reformation,* May/June, 1996, 13.

3. If you are new to Scripture memory, the Topical Memory System developed by the Navigators is an excellent place to begin.

Exercises

Review

1. List and briefly describe five things you are "supposed to do" with Scripture.

2. Explain the biblical concept of *hearing* the Word of God.

3. Why should you resist the temptation to read the Bible in disconnected chunks?

4. Briefly outline an effective approach to studying the Bible. (Hint: What three questions do good Bible students seek to answer?)

5. Read Psalms 118:6–9; 119:11, 105; 1 Corinthians 15:58; Ephesians 2:8–10; and 1 John 3:1–3. Based on these verses, what are some good reasons to memorize Scripture? Can you think of any others?

6. Describe what it means to meditate on Scripture. Support your answer with Scripture.

Application

1. List some ways you (personally) can increase your exposure to hearing the Word of God.

   Now, list several practical ways you (personally) can increase the effectiveness of your listening skills.

2. Distinguish between reading and studying the Bible. Do you read the Bible consistently and regularly? If so, describe your reading plan. If not, find a reading plan you like and begin using it. Do you study the Bible consistently and regularly? If so, describe your study methods. If not, purchase or borrow a copy of *Turning On the Light* and begin learning how to study Scripture.

3. Do you memorize Scripture? If so, describe the methods you use and some of the ways the Holy Spirit has used Scripture memory to help you grow spiritually. (Give specific examples, please.) If not, purchase the Navigator Topical Memory System and begin using it, or consult with a mature Christian who is willing to help you develop a memory system of your own.

4. Describe the meditation of your heart by honestly (and specifically) answering the following questions: (1) What kinds of things do you carry around in your mind? (2) Where do your thoughts tend to wander? (3) If your daydreams were made into a movie, would you allow your children to see it? Is the meditation of your heart acceptable in God's sight? If not, make a detailed plan to change the meditation of your heart and share it with someone who loves you enough to hold you accountable for following through with your plan.

Digging Deeper

1. Explain how hearing, reading, studying, and memorizing Scripture influences the meditation of your heart. Cite appropriate verses to support your reasoning.

2. Do you think our cultural addiction to noise and aversion to serious reading are related in any way? If so, please explain.

3. Explain the connection between Christian unity, biblical wisdom, and kingdom service. Support your reasoning with Scripture and illustrate your explanation with personal examples if possible.

What Must I Do to Be Saved?

A strange sound drifted through the Philippian jail as midnight approached. The sound of human voices—but not the expected groans of the two men who had earlier been beaten with rods and fastened in stocks. Rather, the peaceful singing of praises to their God.

While the other prisoners quietly listened to them, the jailer dozed off, content with the bizarre calm generated by these two preachers, who, hours before, had stirred up so much commotion in the city.

Suddenly a deafening roar filled the prison as the ground began to shake violently. Sturdy doors convulsed and popped open. Chains snapped and fell at prisoners' feet. Startled into full wakefulness, the jailer stared at the wide-open doors and realized his prisoners' certain escape guaranteed his own impending death. Under Roman law, jailers paid with their lives when prisoners escaped. Resolutely, he drew his sword, thinking it better to die by his own hand than by Roman execution.

"Stop! Don't harm yourself—we are all here!" a voice boomed from the darkened inner cell. The jailer called for lights and was astonished to discover his prisoners standing quietly amid their broken chains. Trembling, he rushed in and fell at the feet of the two preachers. As soon as he was able, he led them out of the prison and asked, "Sirs, what must I do to be saved?"

In the entire history of the world, no one has ever asked a more important question. The jailer's words that night may well have been motivated by his critical physical need, but the response of Paul and Silas addressed his even more critical spiritual need: "Believe in the Lord Jesus, and you shall be saved, you and your household" (Acts 16:31).[1]

If you have never "believed in the Lord Jesus," your spiritual need, just like the jailer's, is critical. As long as your life is stained with sin, God cannot receive you into His presence. The Bible says that sin has placed a separation between you and God (Isaiah 59:2). It goes on to say that your nature has been so permeated by sin that you no longer have any desire to serve and obey God (Romans 3:10–12); therefore, you are not likely to recognize or care that a separation exists. Your situation is truly desperate because those who are separated from God will spend eternity in hell.

Since sinful hearts are unresponsive to God, the only way sinners can be saved from their desperate situation is for God to take the initiative. And this He has done! Even though all men and women deserve the punishment of hell because of their sin, God's love has prompted Him to save some who will serve Him in obedience. He did this by sending His Son, the Lord Jesus Christ, to remove the barrier of sin between God and His chosen ones (Colossians 2:13–14).

What is there about Jesus that enables Him to do this? First of all, He is God. While He was on earth, He said, "He who has seen Me has seen the Father" (John 14:9), and "I and the Father are one" (John 10:30). Because He said these things, you must conclude one of three things about His true identity: (1) He was a lunatic who believed He was God when He really wasn't; (2) He was a liar who was willing to die a hideous death for what He knew was a lie; or (3) His words are true and He is God.

Lunatics don't live the way Jesus did, and liars don't die the way He did, so if the Bible's account of Jesus' life and words is true, you can be sure He *is* God.

Since Jesus is God, He is perfectly righteous and holy. God's perfect righteousness and holiness demands that sin be punished (Ezekiel 18:4), and Jesus' perfect righteousness and holiness qualified Him to bear the punishment for the sins of those who will be saved (Romans 6:23). Jesus is the only human who never committed a sin; therefore, the punishment He bore when He died on the cross could be accepted by God as satisfaction of His justice in regard to the sins of others.

If someone you love commits a crime and is sentenced to die, you may offer to die in his place. However, if you have also committed crimes worthy of death, your death cannot satisfy the law's demands for your crimes *and* your loved one's. You can only die in his place if you are innocent of any wrongdoing.

Since Jesus lived a perfect life, God's justice could be satisfied by allowing Him to die for the sins of those who will be saved. Because God is perfectly righteous and holy, He could not act in love at the expense of justice. By sending Jesus to die, God demonstrated His love *by acting to satisfy His own justice* (Romans 3:26).

Jesus did more than die, however. He also rose from the dead. By raising Jesus from the dead, God declared that He had accepted Jesus' death in the place of those who will be saved. Because Jesus lives eternally with God, those for whom Jesus died can be assured they will also spend eternity in heaven (John 14:1–3). The separation of sin has been removed!

Ah, but the all-important question remains unanswered: What must *you do* to be saved? If God has sent His Son into the world for sinners, and Jesus Christ has died in their place, what is left for you to do? You must respond in faith to what God has done. This is what Paul meant when he told the jailer, "Believe in the Lord Jesus, and you shall be saved."

Believing in the Lord Jesus demands three responses from you: (1) an understanding of the facts regarding your hopeless sinful condition and God's action to remove the sin barrier that separates you from Him; (2) acceptance of those facts as true and applicable to you; and (3) a willingness to trust and depend upon God to save you from sin. This involves willingly placing yourself under His authority and acknowledging His sovereign right to rule over you.

But, you say, how can I do this if sin has eliminated my ability to know and appreciate God's work on my behalf? Rest assured that if you desire to have the sin barrier that separates you from God removed, He is already working to change your natural inability to respond. He is extending His gracious offer of salvation to you and will give you the faith to receive it.

If you believe God is working to call you to Himself, read the words He has written to you in the Bible (begin with the book of John in the New Testament) and pray that His Holy Spirit will help you understand what is written there. Continue to read and pray until you are ready to *repent,* that is, to turn away from sin and commit yourself to serving God.

Is there any other way you can be saved? God Himself says no, there is not. The Bible He wrote says that Jesus is the only way the sin barrier between you and God can be removed (John 14:6; Acts 4:12). He is your hope, and He is your *only* hope.

If you have questions or need any help in this matter, please write to The Evangelism Team, Providence Presbyterian Church, P. O. Box 14651, Albuquerque, NM 87191, before the day is over. God has said in His Bible that a day of judgment is coming, and after that day no one will be saved (Acts 17:30–31; 2 Thessalonians 1:7–9). The time to act is now.

Notes

1. See Acts 16:11–40 for the full biblical account of these events.

APPENDIX B

What Is the Reformed Faith?

"The Reformed faith"[1] can be defined as a theology that describes and explains the sovereign God's revelation of His actions in history to glorify Himself by redeeming selected men and women from the just consequences of their self-inflicted depravity.

It is first and foremost *theology* (the study of God), not *anthropology* (the study of humanity). Reformed thinking concentrates on developing a true knowledge of God that serves as the necessary context for all other knowledge. It affirms that the created world, including humanity itself, cannot be accurately understood apart from its relationship with the Creator.

The Reformed faith describes and explains God's revelation of Himself and His actions to humanity; it does not consist of people's attempts to define God as they wish. The Reformed faith asserts that God has revealed Himself in two distinct ways. He reveals His existence, wisdom, and power through the created universe—a process known as *natural revelation* (Romans 1:18–32); and He reveals His requirements and plans for mankind through His written Word, the Bible—a process known as *special revelation* (2 Timothy 3:16–17).

Reformed theologians uphold the Bible as the inspired, infallible, inerrant, authoritative, and fully sufficient communication of truth from God to us. When they say the Bible is "inspired," they mean that the Bible was actually written by God through the agency of human authorship in a miraculous way that preserved the thoughts of God from any taint of human sinfulness (2 Peter 1:20–21).

When they say the Bible is infallible, they mean it is *incapable* of error, and when they say it is inerrant, they mean the Bible, *in actual fact,* contains no errors. The Bible is authoritative because it comes from God whose authority over His creation is absolute (Isaiah 46:9–10). And it is completely sufficient because it contains everything necessary for us to know and live according to God's requirements (2 Peter 1:3–4).

By studying God's revelation of Himself and His work, Reformed theologians have learned two foundational truths that structure their thinking about God's relationship with human beings: God is absolutely sovereign, and people are totally depraved.[2]

Reformed thought affirms that God, by definition, is *absolutely sovereign*—that is, He controls and superintends every circumstance of life either by direct miraculous intervention or by the ordinary outworking of His providence. Reformed theologians understand that a "god" who is not sovereign cannot be God because his power would not be absolute. Since the Reformed faith accepts the Bible's teaching regarding the sovereignty of God, it denies that *anything* occurs outside of God's control.

The Reformed faith affirms the biblical teaching that Adam was created with the ability to sin and chose to do so by disobeying a clear command of God (Genesis 3:1–7). Choosing to sin changed basic human nature and left us unable not to sin—or *totally depraved*. Total depravity does not mean that all people are as bad as they possibly could be, but that every facet of their character is tainted with sin, leaving them incapable and undesirous of fellowship with God. The Reformed faith denies that totally depraved men and women have any ability to seek after or submit to God of their own free will. Left to themselves, totally depraved men and women will remain out of fellowship with God for all eternity.

The only way for any of these men and women to have their fellowship with God restored is for God Himself to take the initiative. And the Bible declares that He has graciously chosen to do so (John 14:16). *For His own glory,* God has chosen some of those depraved men and women to live in fellowship with Him. His choice is determined by His own good pleasure and not by any virtue in the ones He has chosen. For this reason, *grace* is defined in Reformed thought as "unmerited favor."

God accomplished the salvation of His chosen ones by sending His Son, the Lord Jesus Christ, to bear God's righteous wrath against sin so that He could forgive those He had chosen. Even though Christ's work was perfect and complete, its effectiveness is limited to those who are chosen by God for salvation. Christ would not have been required to suffer any more or any less had a different number been chosen for redemption, but the benefit of His suffering is applied only to those who are called by God to believe in Him.

All of those who are thus effectually called by God will eventually believe and be saved, even though they may resist for a time (John 6:37). They cannot forfeit the salvation they have received (John 10:27–30; Romans 8:31–39).

Reformed thought affirms the clear teaching of the Bible that salvation is by faith alone through Christ alone (John 14:6; Acts 4:12; Ephesians 2:8–9), and that our good works play no part in salvation although they are generated by it (Ephesians 2:10). Salvation transforms a person's nature, giving him or her the ability and the desire to serve and obey God. The unresponsive heart of stone is changed into a sensitive heart of flesh that responds readily to God's voice (Ezekiel 36:25–27) and desires to glorify Him out of gratitude for the indescribable gift of salvation.

Reformed thought affirms that *God works in history to redeem* His chosen ones through a series of covenants. These covenants define His law, assess penalties for breaking His law, and provide for the imputation of Jesus' vicarious fulfillment of God's requirements to those God intends to redeem.[3]

The Reformed faith affirms that we were created and exist solely to glorify God, and denies that God exists to serve us. It affirms that God acts to glorify Himself by putting His attributes on display, and that His self-glorifying actions are thoroughly righteous since He is the only Being in creation worthy of glorification. It denies that God is *primarily* motivated to act by man's needs, but affirms that all of God's actions are motivated *primarily* for His own glory.

The Reformed faith emerged as a distinct belief system during the sixteenth and seventeenth centuries when men like Luther, Calvin, Zwingli, and Knox fought against the Roman Catholic

Church to restore Christian doctrine to biblical truth. These men were labeled "Reformers," but they would have been better labeled "Restorers" since their goal was to correct abuses and distortions of Christianity that were rampant in the established Roman church. Reformed thinkers since their day have sought to align their understanding of God and His actions in history as closely as possible to His revealed truth.

Notes

1. This brief overview of basic Reformed beliefs is not intended to be a full explanation of or apologetic for the Reformed faith. For a more detailed description and analysis of the Reformed faith see: R. C. Sproul, *Grace Unknown* (Grand Rapids: Baker, 1997), Loraine Boettner, *The Reformed Faith* (Phillipsburg, N.J.: Presbyterian and Reformed, 1983), *Back to Basics: Rediscovering the Richness of the Reformed Faith,* ed. David G. Hagopian (Phillipsburg, N.J.: P&R Publishing, 1996), *The Westminster Confession of Faith* (with its accompanying catechisms), or the theological writings of John Calvin, B. B. Warfield, Charles Hodge, and Louis Berkhof.

2. Both of these truths are taught throughout the pages of Scripture; however, the sovereignty of God can be seen very clearly in Isaiah 40–60 and in Job 38–42, while human depravity is described quite graphically in Romans 3:10–18.

3. An excellent discussion of these covenants is contained in chapter 5 of R. C. Sproul, *Grace Unknown.*

The Chicago Statement on Biblical Inerrancy

The Summary Statement

1. God, who is himself truth and speaks truth only, has inspired Holy Scripture in order thereby to reveal himself to lost mankind through Jesus Christ as Creator and Lord, Redeemer and Judge. Holy Scripture is God's witness to himself.

2. Holy Scripture, being God's own Word, written by men prepared and superintended by his Spirit, is of infallible divine authority in all matters upon which it touches: it is to be believed, as God's instruction, in all that it affirms; obeyed, as God's command, in all that it requires; embraced, as God's pledge, in all that it promises.

3. The Holy Spirit, Scripture's divine author, both authenticates it to us by his inward witness and opens our minds to understand its meaning.

4. Being wholly and verbally God-given, Scripture is without error or fault in all its teaching, no less in what it states about God's acts in creation, about the events of world history, and about its own literary origins under God, than in its witness to God's saving grace in individual lives.

5. The authority of Scripture is inescapably impaired if this total divine inerrancy is in any way limited or disregarded, or made relative to a view of truth contrary to the Bible's own; and such lapses bring serious loss to both the individual and the church.

RECOMMENDED READING

Adler, Mortimer J., and Charles Van Doren. *How to Read a Book.* New York: Simon and Schuster, 1972.

Boice, James Montgomery. *Standing on the Rock: Biblical Authority in a Secular Age.* Grand Rapids: Baker, 1994.

Bruce, F. F. *The Canon of Scripture.* Downers Grove, Ill.: InterVarsity Press, 1988.

Hendricks, Howard G., and William D. Hendricks. *Living by the Book.* Chicago: Moody Press, 1991.

Kistler Don, ed. *Sola Scriptura! The Protestant Position on the Bible.* Morgan, Pa.: Soli Deo Gloria, 1995.

Linnemann, Eta. *Historical Criticism of the Bible: Methodology or Ideology?* Translated by Robert W. Yarbrough. Grand Rapids: Baker, 1990.

MacArthur, John, Jr. *Our Sufficiency in Christ.* Dallas: Word, 1991.

———. *The Silent Shepherd.* Wheaton, Ill.: Victor, 1996.

———. *How to Get the Most from God's Word.* Dallas: Word, 1997.

Packer, J. I. *God Has Spoken.* Grand Rapids: Baker, 1979.

———. *Fundamentalism and the Word of God.* Grand Rapids: Eerdmans, 1958, 1983.

Pink, Arthur W. *The Holy Spirit.* Grand Rapids: Baker, 1970.

Postman, Neil. *Amusing Ourselves to Death.* New York: Penguin Books, 1985.

Sproul, R. C. *The Mystery of the Holy Spirit.* Wheaton, Ill.: Tyndale House, 1990.

Warfield, Benjamin B. *The Inspiration and Authority of the Bible.* Edited by Samuel G. Craig. Philadelphia: Presbyterian and Reformed, 1948.